Group Work:
Creating Space for All Voices

Proceedings of the XXXVII International Symposium
of the International Association for Social Work with Groups,
Chapel Hill, North Carolina, USA, June 4-7, 2015

Group Work
Creating Space for All Voices

Edited by
Lorrie Greenhouse Gardella and Greg Tully

w&b

MMXIX

© Whiting & Birch Ltd 2019

Published by Whiting & Birch Ltd
Forest Hill, London SE23 3HZ

ISBN 9781861771469

Contents

The XXXVII International Symposium
of the International Association for Social Work with Groups,
Chapel Hill, North Carolina, USA, June 4-7, 2015

Acknowledgements

**The XXXVII International Symposium
of the International Association for Social Work with
Groups,Chapel Hill, North Carolina, USA, June 4-7, 2015**

2015 IASWG Honoree
Nancy Sullivan

Symposium Local Honorees:
Roberta Wallace
Karla Siu
Jodi Flick
Larry Bernstein

Symposium Co-Chairs
Anne C. Jones, Marilyn Ann Ghezzi, and Willa J. Casstevens

IASWG Symposium Planner
Emily Wilk

The 2015 IASWG Symposium was supported by the University of North Carolina at Chapel Hill and the North Carolina State School of Social Work, especially Jack M. Richman, Ph.D., professor and dean, UNC School of Social Work; and Karen Bullock, Ph.D., professor and head of the department of Social Work, North Carolina State University. Thank you! The assistance from both universities created a wonderful collaboration.

Special thanks to Emily Wilk (IASWG Symposium Planner) for going beyond what was asked to strengthen the event planning. Thanks also to the student volunteers from the various schools of social work, and to the IASWG Board members, all of whom were supportive and helpful to the work of the symposium.

Thank you to the many authors in this volume who contributed their scholarly writing. Much appreciation from those of us in IASWG for your participation in this publishing project. Thank you to Natalie Shriefer for proofreading.

And lastly, a special thank you to David Whiting, our IASWG publisher. Without his guidance and support we could not have developed and produced this volume.

Dedication

Maeda J. Galinsky, Courtesy of UNC School of Social Work

The 37th Annual IASWG Symposium was held on the campus of the University of North Carolina at Chapel Hill from June 4 to 7, 2015. Just one day earlier, on June 3, the UNC School of Social work celebrated the retirement of Maeda J. Galinksy, Keenan Distinguished Professor Emerita, who had served on the faculty for 50 years. The symposium planning committee recognized Professor Galinksy as an Honored Group Work Leader in light of her contributions to group work education, research, and practice and her decades of service and leadership in IASWG.

The editors are pleased to dedicate this volume of the IASWG Proceedings to Maeda Galinsky, and we invited her UNC faculty colleagues Anne Jones and Marilyn Ghezzi to offer a brief tribute and to select one of her publications for inclusion as the opening chapter.

About the Editors

Lorrie Greenhouse Gardella, JD, LMSW, ACSW, is associate professor of Social Work and MSW program coordinator at Southern Connecticut State University in New Haven, Connecticut, USA. Introduced to social group work as a settlement house volunteer, she served as a consultant in children's law before earning her MSW degree. Gardella has published in the areas of social group work, social work with migrants, and social work history, including the acclaimed biography, *The Life and Thought of Louis Lowy: Social Work through the Holocaust* (Syracuse University Press, 2011). Having held leadership positions in various social work associations, she is proud to serve as a member-at-large on the IASWG Board of Directors. Email: lggardella@gmail.com

Greg Tully, Ph.D., MSW is a professor in Social Work at West Chester University in Pennsylvania, USA. He also teaches courses for the Silver School of Social Work at New York University, has been a faculty member at both Iona College and Barry University, and has taught courses at the Hunter College Silberman School of Social Work. He has presented internationally, and published books and articles, including contributions to the *Encyclopedia of Social Work with Groups, the Journal of Teaching in Social Work, Groupwork,* and *Social Work with Groups.* He is President of the International Association for Social Work with Groups. Email: gtully@wcupa.edu.

The Contributors

Willa J. Casstevens, PhD, MSW, LCSW, is Associate Professor at the North Carolina State University Department of Social Work in Raleigh, North Carolina, USA. Prior to coming to NC State in 2006, she practiced in south Florida's community mental health arena for approximately fifteen years. She was principal investigator with Dr. Jodi Hall on the Garrett Lee Smith (GLS) Campus Suicide Prevention Grant at NC State. Her research involves prevention and alternative approaches to intervention in mental health. She is a longtime member of IASWG. Email: wjcasste@ncsu.edu

Carol S. Cohen, MSW, DSW, is a faculty member of Adelphi University School of Social Work, New York, USA. She is an IASWG board member, co-chair of IASWG Group's Commission on Group Work in Social Work Education, and a Fulbright Scholar. She is co-chair, Council of Social Work Education's Group Work Track, and past chair of CSWE's Commission on Global Social Work Education. Her publications span local and international group work, social work education, and community development. Her most recent book, *Practicing as a Social Work Educator in International Collaboration,* with Alice Butterfield, was published by CSWE Press in 2017. Email: cohen5@adelphi.edu

Mark Doel, Ph.D., MA (Oxon), CQSW, is professor emeritus in the Centre for Health and Social Care Research at Sheffield Hallam University, England. He is a registered social worker with twenty years of direct practice experience with communities, specializing in group work. He has been a social work teacher and trainer, a head of school, and a writer and researcher. He leads training workshops, largely in the fields of groupwork and practice education, and he continues to be an external examiner for social work programmes and doctoral candidates. He has extensive experience in Russia and Eastern Europe and he is honorary professor at Tbilisi State University, Georgia. Doel has published widely, including 21 books, most recently *Social Work in 42 Objects (and more),* and *Rights and Wrongs in Social Work: Ethical and practice dilemmas.* He is the Vice-President of the International Association for Social Work with Groups (IASWG). Email: doel@waitrose.com

Maeda J. Galinksy, Ph.D., MSW, is Keenan Distinguished Professor Emerita in the University of North Carolina School of Social Work, where she taught social group work practice for 50 years. She authored and co-authored numerous articles on group work theory and practice, and she edited and wrote pivotal books on group work and intervention research. She was the co-principal investigator of the Making Choices Project, an intervention program aimed at preventing violence and aggression in children. She served on the IASWG Board of Directors for many years. Email: maeda@email.unc.edu

Marilyn Ghezzi, MSW, LCSW, is clinical assistant professor at the University of North Carolina at Chapel Hill, where she teaches courses on mental health theory and practice, group work, differential diagnosis, and other mental health topics. She has won numerous teaching awards including the 2017 Distinguished Teaching Award for Post-baccalaureate Instruction. Prior to joining the faculty in 2008, she worked as a clinical social worker in the public mental health system for 24 years. She continues to practice as a clinical social worker, including provision of clinical supervision to mental health professionals. She is a member of IASWG. Email: mghezzi@email.unc.edu

Alexis Howard, LCSW-R, is the immediate past coordinator of the New York City Social Work Education Consortium, under the auspices of the University at Albany, where her work focused on supporting the professionalization and the transfer of learning for the New York City public child welfare workforce. She is currently functioning in a similar capacity under the Administration for Children's Services (ACS) Workforce Institute, and she was instrumental in the professionalization of the New York City Department of Homeless Services workforce members. She is currently a social welfare doctoral student at the Graduate Center, City University of New York; a board member-at-large of the International Association for Social Work with Groups; and a member of the ACS Racial Equity and Cultural Competence committee. Email: Alexis.Howard@acs.nyc.gov

Anne C. Jones, Ph.D., MSW, is a clinical professor at the University of North Carolina at Chapel Hill. Her primary clinical and research interests include prevention of chronic mental health problems, couple and family relationships, group work, and integrated health care. She currently is co-directing the UNC Prime Care Program, a grant from the Substance Abuse and Mental Health Services Administration. She is a licensed clinical social worker and teaches direct practice courses. She holds a MSW from the University of Pittsburgh and a Ph.D. from Simmons College. Email: annejone@email.unc.edu

Patricia Ki, RSW, RCAT, PhD Cand., is a doctoral student in the Critical Disability Studies at York University, Toronto. She is also a registered art therapist and social worker, and has been working in the area of women's mental health since 2010. Email: ki.patricia@gmail.com

Andrew Malekoff, LCSW, CASAC, is executive director of North Shore Child and Family Guidance Center in Roslyn Heights, New York, where he has worked for more than 40 years. He entered the human services field as a Volunteer in Service to America in Grand Island, Nebraska in 1974, an experience that inspired him to pursue his MSW degree. A prolific writer, he is editor of the journal, *Social Work with Groups* and author of the acclaimed *Group Work with Adolescents: Principles and practice*, 3rd Edition (Guilford Press, 2014). He serves on the Board of Directors of IASWG. Email: Anjru@aol.com or amalekoff@northshorechildguidance.org

Kyle McGee, MSW, LMSW, is a licensed social worker with over twenty years of experience as a clinician, supervisor, educator, and trainer. Co-recipient of the NASW Emerging Leadership Award in 2009, Kyle's practice has focused on individual and group mental health treatment with children and adults. He currently is employed by the New York University Langone Medical Center as a trainer and implementation coordinator for ParentCorps, a community-based initiative for Pre-K aged children and their families. A doctoral student at Adelphi University, he has served as an adjunct professor at Adelphi University and the Silberman School of Social Work at Hunter College. He has developed curriculum and incorporated the use of music and drumming into his practice with groups. He serves as co-chair of the Nominations and Membership Committee on the IASWG Board of Directors. Email: kylem.mcgee@gmail.com

Karen Miller, MSW, BS, is the Director of Project Management at 3C Institute in Durham, North Carolina, USA. 3C Institute delivers custom software services to improve social, emotional, and behavioral health. Miller has developed online applications that measure youth social-emotional health, monitor fidelity adherence in program implementation, and disseminate clinical training through interactive courses. Prior to working with 3C, she was the Program Coordinator for the Garrett Lee Smith (GLS) Campus Suicide Prevention Grant at North Carolina State University Department of Social Work. Email: kmiller@3cisd.com

Adina Muskat, MA, MSW, RSW, is a registered social worker in Toronto, Canada. She is currently working in a supportive housing program in downtown Toronto with women living with mental health and substance use challenges. She previously worked in hospital settings, in children's mental health, and in therapeutic residential programs with youth. Email: adinamuskat@gmail.com

Erin Nau, LCSW, is counseling/education coordinator at the Adelphi NY Statewide Breast Cancer Hotline and Support Program, where she counsels individuals and facilitates support groups for women diagnosed with breast cancer. She is field instructor, adjunct professor, and doctoral candidate Adelphi University School of Social Work. Having practiced social work with various populations, including clients with severe and persistent mental illness, families, and adolescents, she has devoted her career to empowering women and girls. She is a member of IASWG and she serves on the Council on Social Work Education (CSWE) Council on the Role and Status of Women in Social Work Education. Email: erinlnau@gmail.com

Natia Partskhaladze, MD, MSc, MSW, is a leader in the area of social protections systems in the country of Georgia. She has 18 years of social work experience, including service in UNICEF Child Protection. As a senior national child protection specialist in Georgia, she provides strategic support to the executive and legislative branches of the Georgian government. She played a key role in planning and implementing preventive and alternative care services within the Georgian child protection system, which led to the deinstitutionalization of thousands of children. She is a founder and chairperson of the Georgian Association of Social Workers (GASW), a professional organization that supports the development and strengthening of the social work profession. She also holds leadership positions in the Global Social Service Workforce Alliance. Partskhaladze is an adjunct professor at Tbilisi State University. E-mail: natia@nilc.org.ge

Janice Hough Schopler, Ph.D., MSW, ACSW, (1941 to 1997) was professor and associate dean at the University of North Carolina School of Social Work, where she taught in the areas of social group work, macro practice, and theory. Her research and writing focused on the development and testing of social interventions, particularly in the areas of social work with groups and inter-organizational systems. She authored and co-authored many books, chapters, and articles on group work theory and practice.

Shirley R. Simon, ACSW, LCSW, is Associate Professor, School of Social Work, Loyola University Chicago, USA. She has been a social work educator for over forty years, chairs the group work sequence within Loyola's School of Social Work, and spearheaded the creation of the Group Work Sub-Specialization which opens fall 2018. She has published on group work education, practice, and history, and has facilitated approximately two hundred student and alumni presentations at professional association conferences. Simon is Book Review Editor for North America for the journal *Groupwork*. She currently serves as member-at-large to the IASWG Board of Directors and she was named 2017 IASWG Honoree. Email: ssimon@luc.edu

Introduction

The theme of the 2015 IASWG Symposium, "Group Work: Creating Space for All Voices," informed more than 100 paper presentations, poster presentations, and panel discussions on the campus of the University of North Carolina at Chapel Hill. The symposium theme invoked the history of social group work with its emphasis on citizenship, democracy, and social justice; the ongoing development of group work as a global and local, macro and micro level profession; and the method of group work as a resource for social and individual action and wellbeing. The nine chapters presented here explore the enduring values of group work as realized in practice today.

This volume of the *Proceedings of the 37th International Symposia on Social Work with Groups* is dedicated to Maeda J. Galinsky, whose retirement from the University of North Carolina coincided with the symposium. Chapter One reprints the classic paper, "Patterns of Entry and Exit in Open-Ended Groups," which Galinksy and Janice H. Schopler first presented in 1983 at the fifth Annual Symposium of what was then AASWG (the Association for the Advancement of Social Work with Groups). Observing the increasing popularity of open-ended groups, Galinsky and Schopler studied how practitioners respond to fluctuating group membership as they address the various needs of new members, departing members, and continuing members. Based on a sample of 66 groups, the authors concluded that open-ended groups appear to promote individual and group development when practitioners adapt their knowledge and skills to the group's changing contexts and needs.

Social workers negotiate radical social change in Chapter Two, "Groupwork as the Georgian Association of Social Workers' Approach for Promoting Collective Action," by Natia Partskhaladze. A founding member of the Georgian Association of Social Workers (GASW), Partskhaladze examines the introduction and development of professional social work in the newly independent country of Georgia, where traditional family and communitarian values, once challenged by Soviet rule, are now shifting to more individualistic economic priorities. Georgian social workers are using their knowledge and skills as group workers to mediate cultural values, to build international collaborations, and to advocate with the national government for social system reforms.

The accomplishments of the Georgian Association of Social Workers are consistent with the exemplary case studies presented in Chapter 3, *"Actualizing the Global Agenda for Social Work and Social Development through Social Group Work,"* by Carol Cohen, Alexis Howard, Kyle McGee, and Erin Nau. As the first phase of a broader international study, this chapter examines four human services agencies in the greater New York metropolitan area that use group work to deliver services, to support staff members, and to lead organizations. Group work promotes the Global Agenda (IASSW, ICSW, IFSW, 2012) within and without organizations by attending to the principles of social and economic equality, human dignity and worth, environmental and community sustainability, and the importance of human relationships.

To Andrew Malekoff, who serves as executive director of North Shore Child and Family Guidance Center (one of the organizations that is profiled in Chapter 3), group work is a coherent yet chaotic process. "As a group worker, what I know is that it is often the frenetic kid's group that has more order to it, a method to the madness, if you will, than the rational, tightly controlled, and superficially polite business or faculty meeting . . ." In Chapter 4, "On Getting Over Oneself and Creating Space for All Voices in Group Work With Adolescents," Malekoff assumes a stance of uncertainty, an ability to listen, and a willingness to lose control. Effective group workers are guided more by the creativity and wisdom of group members than by the evidence-based prescriptions of formal research.

It is group members, rather than experts, who best understand and support one another in Chapter 5, "A Place in History: Adelphi NY Statewide Breast Cancer Hotline and Support Program" by Erin Nau. In 1980, when breast cancer was not openly discussed in families and communities, a post-mastectomy support group allowed women to break their silence, build confidence, and provide voluntary services to other survivors. Based on archival and personal testimony research, Nau profiles the development of the breast cancer support program from its early support groups, to specialized groups, to open-ended groups that meet survivors' ongoing needs.

In Chapter 6, "A Group Work Challenge to Maintain Group Purpose in an Open-Ended Group," Adina Muskat describes opportunities and challenges in her practice with an open-ended bariatric surgery support group. As anticipated by Galinksy and Schloper in Chapter 1, the open-ended support group searches for its purpose while trying to address members' particular concerns. It is only after group members accept their differences, that they are able to affirm their common goals.

Focus groups reveal students' perspectives on suicide in Chapter 7, "Using Focus Groups to Inform Suicide Prevention Efforts on Campus" by Willa J. Casstevens and Karen J. Miller. The authors recruited students from three higher risk populations – students in Greek Life, students in LGBT communities, and undergraduates – to gain their insights on improving engagement and awareness in an existing suicide prevention program. The focus groups shared several recommendations as well as raising an unexpected issue, the importance of combatting stigma in the promotion of community mental health.

Social work students find their professional voices in Chapter 8, "Professional Development: An MSW Course Based on Group Work Principles and Opportunities" by Shirley R. Simon. A model professional development seminar harnesses the power of mutual aid as students facilitate class discussions, prepare professional development projects, and participate in a professional conference. The seminar supports students in defining their goals as they form their individual and shared identities as social workers.

In contrast to students who are looking forward to their careers, James A. Garland reflects back on his professional development in Chapter 9, "Remembering Jim Garland: Loneliness in the Group," by Lorrie Greenhouse Gardella. Based on oral history interviews that were conducted at the time of his retirement from Boston University School of Social Work, Garland's life story is presented in phases similar to those of his well-known model of group development (Garland, Jones, & Kolodny, 1965). Once attentive to the connection and closeness experienced by group members, Garland now is concerned with their inevitable separation. In ending his career, as in ending his groups, he takes comfort in the "forever transitional object" that is the social work profession.

References

Garland, J. A.; Jones, H. E.; & Kolodny, R. L. (1965). A model for stages of development in social work groups. In S. Bernstein (Ed.), *Explorations in Group Work* (pp. 17-71). Boston, MA: Charles River Books.

IASSW, ICSW, IFSW (2012). *Global agenda for social work and social development: Commitment to action.* Retrieved from http://cdn.ifsw.org/assets/globalagenda2012.pdf

A Tribute to Maeda J. Galinsky

Marilyn Ann Ghezzi and Anne C. Jones

Maeda J. Galinsky, Ph.D., MSW, Kenan Distinguished Professor Emerita in the University of North Carolina School of Social Work, retired in 2015 after 50 years of outstanding scholarly service. Despite the passage of time and the tremendous social changes over these many decades, Maeda continues to impact the social work profession and specifically the practice of group work. Throughout her career, she was a remarkable academic who was able to do it all and to do so with passion, grace, humor, and humility. She was an excellent instructor, researcher, author, mentor, colleague, and friend. She is also a mother of three children and devoted spouse to her beloved David. Maeda continues to possess that rare combination of seemingly boundless energy, intellectual curiosity, warmth, and compassion that seems to affect all those around her.

Our biggest challenge in writing this tribute was choosing just one article to be reprinted in this volume that would represent a career's worth of work. Maeda wrote with the intention of having an impact on both the academic and practitioner community. Her work, often in collaboration with her dear friend and colleague Janice H. Schopler, was research-based and driven. She held high standards for herself and others and the result was a body of work that continues to be relevant and ahead of its time.

The article we chose to highlight is entitled, "Patterns of Entry and Exit in Open-Ended Groups," originally presented at the 5th Annual Symposium of AASWG in 1983 and published in *Social Work with Groups* in 1985. Maeda and Jan's work on open-ended groups in the 1980s shows how they were continually breaking new ground. At that time, the current thinking on group development was largely based on the research of Garland, Jones, and Kolodny (1965) and Tuckman and Jensen (1977), which focused on closed therapeutic groups. Maeda and Jan developed a group development typology that took into account the reality of membership turnover seen in most groups. The publications, "Patterns of Entry and Exit in Open-Ended Groups" (1985) and "Developmental Patterns of Open-Ended Groups" (1989) were empirically-based and practical in nature. This work helped practitioners like ourselves better understand and respond to the more typical patterns of development in the groups that we have led.

"Patterns of Entry and Exit in Open-Ended Groups" demonstrates Maeda's reliance on research to support or dispute her assumptions. The article's exploration of open-ended groups was based on a survey of 55 local social workers, resulting in a robust sample of 66 open-ended groups. The other salient characteristic of Maeda's work exemplified by this article is its practicality and connection to the practice world. Throughout her career, Maeda was interested in group work practice. She wanted not only to help to improve practice but also to learn from practitioners.

Several other articles could have been selected based on these same qualities. "Connecting Group Members through Telephone and Computer Groups" appeared in the journal *Health and Social Work* in 1997. Maeda was lead author and co-authors were Jan Schopler and Melissa D. Abell. The fact that this article was written more than two decades ago exemplifies Maeda's forward thinking. In the mid-nineties, relatively few practitioners were facilitating technology-based groups and even fewer practitioners or academics were writing about them.

In 2006, Maeda was once again ahead of the curve as lead author with Mary A. Terzian and Mark W. Fraser of "The Art of Group Work Practice with Manualized Curricula" in *Social Work with Groups*. Manualized groups were only beginning to be acknowledged by some parts of the group work community as a legitimate group work method due to concerns that this format was mechanical and devoid of spontaneity and feeling. As usual, Maeda was out in front. She wanted to help others see that group facilitators could lead groups that were replicable and evidence-based without compromising creativity and compassion.

Finally, we would be remiss not to mention Maeda's and Jan's 1977 article, "Warning: Groups may be Dangerous" which appeared in *Social Work*. This paper was not only far-sighted and empirically-based, but it was, like Maeda, honest and courageous. It describes the kinds of risks and negative outcomes that can and do occur in groups. Although written more than forty years ago, this article remains relevant and, we would argue, should be required reading for direct practice MSW students.

We want to close by noting several other aspects of Maeda that we have both cherished over the years. In addition to being an intellectual leader and researcher, Maeda possessed attributes that were not necessarily obvious to those outside of her home institution. Throughout her career, Maeda was unusually kind and supportive to students and colleagues. She kept in touch with students after they graduated and continued not only to encourage them but also to learn from them. This was but one of many ways that she stayed close to the practice world. Maeda delighted in the role of mentor and was always willing to make time to serve as a sounding board, to edit the work of others, and to help generate ideas for papers and abstracts. We have both been the recipient of Maeda's kindness, generosity, wisdom, and yes, even the red marks of her edits. We are grateful for this opportunity to share our experiences of her with others.

References

Galinsky, M. J. & Schopler, J. H. (1989). Developmental patterns in open-ended groups. *Social Work with Groups*, 12(2), 99-114, Doi: 10.1300/J009v12n02_08

Galinsky, M. J., & Schopler, J. H. (1977). Warning: Groups may be dangerous. *Social Work*, 22(2), 89.

Galinsky, M. J., Schopler, J. H., & Abell, M. D. (1997). Connecting group members through telephone and computer groups. *Health and Social Work*, 22(3), 181-188. doi:10.1093/hsw/22.3.181

Galinsky, M. J., Terzian, M. A., Fraser, M. W. (2006). The art of group work practice with manualized curricula. *Social Work with Groups*, 29(1), 11-26. DOI: 10.1300/J009v29n01_03

Galinsky, M. J. & Schopler, J. H. (1985). Patterns of entry and exit in open-ended groups. *Social Work with Groups*, 8(2), 67-80. DOI: 10.1300/Joo9v08n02_07

Garland, J. A; Jones, H. E.; & Kolodny, R .L. (1965). A model for stages of development in social work groups. In S. Bernstein (Ed.), *Explorations in Group Work* (pp. 17-71). Boston: Charles River Books.

Tuckman, B. W., & Jensen, M. A. (1977). Stages of small group development revisited. *Group and Organization Studies*, 2, 419-42

Patterns of Entry and Exit in Open-Ended Groups

Maeda J. Galinsky and Janice H. Schopler

Abstract: This descriptive study of 66 open-ended groups identifies characteristics and patterns found in open group systems. While the groups endure over time, members typically stay for only brief periods. Membership change, the dominant feature of these groups, is associated with the frequent use of systematic procedures for member entry and exit. These procedures, designed to maintain group stability and speed member integration, offer useful guidance to practitioners coping with ongoing and often unpredictable change in open-ended groups.

Introduction

Open-ended groups represent a unique time perspective. The group system endures over time, but the tenure of individual members is typically brief. The open-ended group is designed to offer an immediate, ongoing response to client needs; members can enter and depart on a continuous basis without waiting until a new group is formed. The time-limited pattern of membership is determined by several factors. Length of stay may be dictated by the focus of the group, as in orientation groups; by the boundaries of contact with an agency, as in groups for parents of hospitalized children; by fulfillment of a court order, as in groups for spouse abusers; by achievement of personal goals, as in therapy groups for mothers of preschool children; or, by temporary member need for crisis counseling and support, as in groups for relatives of newly diagnosed Alzheimer's disease patients. While some members contract beforehand for the number of sessions they will attend, the period of participation is often unpredictable, either because member relationships with the organization are variable, or because some members achieve their purposes more rapidly than others.

Because of the frequent turnover, circumscribed stay, and

unpredictability of membership, there is a need to focus quickly on the task to ensure that members receive the services intended. Members know their time together may be brief. Some members may come for only one session and many attend less than five meetings. For current members to see results, each session must be productive.

A constant feature of open-ended groups is the ever-present possibility of member entry or exit. While frequency of membership change varies, each time a new member is added or an old one leaves, the group must adapt to the change in composition. At the same time that open membership provides a necessary flexibility, it also leads to a disruption of the group process and creates a challenge for the practitioner, requiring new conceptual and practice tools to cope with these perpetual changes.

The questions of practitioners seeking more effective ways to contend with continual member entry and exit prompted our interest in this research. Seeking answers, we reviewed the literature and found extensive reports of varied practitioner experiences with open-ended groups but few theoretical discussions. Existing group theory tends to focus on groups with stable long-term membership and provides little direction for interventions to support ongoing membership change.

Disparate accounts from practice did, however, provide a basis for our beginning conceptualization of openended groups. We identified the purposes, composition, group arrangements, group development, structure, and processes found in the open-ended groups reported in the literature and offered guidelines for intervention (Schopler and Galinsky, 1984).

In this descriptive study of open-ended groups, we are exploring patterns and interventions associated with open membership and the validity of the principles we suggested. The empirical description of current practice is intended to provide a beginning base for the development of theory supporting practitioner efforts. Since our data collection is still in process, we are reporting our preliminary findings as they relate to group characteristics and patterns of member entry and departure and to the practitioner interventions used to deal with membership change. At a later date we will be examining the relationships among patterns, interventions, and the course of group development in our expanded sample.

Method of Study

Our data are derived from questionnaires completed by social work practitioners about the open-ended groups they lead or colead. Open-ended groups are defined by the intent to keep membership open, whether change occurs every meeting or as infrequently as once in six months. To locate respondents, we are polling current and recent field instructors of the School of Social Work of the University of North Carolina by telephone to determine if they are serving open-ended groups and to obtain names of other practitioners leading such groups. The sample to date includes a wide range of groups served in both public and private agencies in central North Carolina.

Respondents are asked to complete a questionnaire designed to elicit information about group purpose, composition, group arrangements, entry of new members, termination of old members, and group development. Further, respondents are asked to give their impressions of the advantages and disadvantages related to open membership in groups and to describe any special procedures they find helpful in their work.

Description of the Respondents

The 55 social workers who completed the questionnaires included in our preliminary analysis represent a total of 66 open-ended groups. The 89% response rate is only tentative since there has not been sufficient time for all questionnaires to be completed and we are still soliciting respondents. Forty-five individuals reported on one group; nine reported on two groups; and one respondent reported on three groups. Three-fourths of the 55 respondents are direct service workers and about three-fifths of them work at in-patient or residential settings. A slight majority of the respondents are in the field of mental health but other areas, such as health, families and children, and aging are also included. Most of these social workers are in settings where the primary focus is on the provision of clinical services with a few in outreach and training organizations or in agencies combining these two functions.

All of the respondents were trained social workers who had at least an MSW, except for one person with a PhD who co-led a group with an MSW. They tended to be experienced practitioners who had some type of formal preparation for group work either through their social work education or other types of training.

Description of the Sample

The current sample consists of 66 groups, all led or co-led by social work professionals. These groups may not be representative of all open-ended groups, but they exemplify the range of groups formed to serve people who have pressing needs on an ongoing basis. They include groups for cancer patients who need continuing support, education about the disease, and coping skills to meet the often devastating consequences for their personal, family, and work lives; groups for adolescents living in group homes who have to deal with issues of group living, of identity, and of family relationships; groups of chronically mentally ill residing in the community and learning to deal with a non-institutional setting, with interpersonal problems, with "dead time," and with the response of others to their condition; and, groups to provide support and help to caregivers in nursing homes, where demanding and sometimes tedious tasks often cause stress and boredom. The groups we examined were located in mental hospitals, general hospitals, community mental health centers, half-way houses for mental patients, group care facilities for youth, child abuse prevention programs and family service agencies, to name but a few. Despite the diversity of these groups, they all have open boundaries and deal with membership change on a continuing basis.

Purposes

The majority of the groups examined were created to provide services to adults, with some groups serving children and adolescents, and a few serving a mixture of both. Most groups were directed to the identified client, whether that was the sole emphasis or also involved significant others in the clients' lives. A few were for significant others only or for staff. Family and individual problems were the primary focus in the majority (59%) of these groups; the remainder of the groups had a primary focus on lack of interpersonal/ task/social skills (18%), need for information (15%), group living issues (5%) and job-stress related problems (3%).

Whatever their primary focus, the groups in our sample addressed a multiplicity of specific purposes to meet member needs. Responses to a checklist of ten possible purposes indicated that 41% of the groups held six or more of these purposes, 45% of the groups held four or five purposes, and 14% addressed two or three purposes. Not a single group was designed to meet only one purpose. The specific purposes were checked with variable frequency: support (94%), problem-solving (88%), education (76%), training for staff and students (68%), treatment (64%), skills training (53%), orientation (36%), advocacy (20%), screening and assessment (18%), and other, including aims such as coordination of services (8%).

Composition

Leadership patterns indicated a predominance of co-leaders: 88% of the groups were led by two or more practitioners. Group size is fairly constant and falls within a narrow range for most groups: 76% of the groups reported an average attendance of 4, 5, 6, or 7 members, with a modal response of 5. Almost all groups could identify such an average attendance. Workers reported that there was considerable variation in attendance from meeting to meeting in about half of the groups, while the other half reported little variation. Of those 35 groups which experienced fluctuations, over half noted that they could expect differences in size of between 1 and 5 persons from meeting to meeting. A modal response of 8 members (26%) was reported for greatest number attending; most groups (70%) had anywhere from 6 to 10 members as their highest attendance.

Potential members were drawn from a number of sources. Members came from staff referrals, from the workers' caseloads, from self-referral, or from advertisements. In addition, members were referred by professionals in related organizations; or were invited to attend because of their particular status (e.g., parent of child in the project, cancer patient, or resident).

Not all potential members were accepted into the groups in the sample; about three-fifths had some type of criteria for member selection or exclusion, and some respondents used multiple criteria to determine membership. Criteria used to screen potential members included common diagnosis or problem; selected characteristics such as age, marital status, and sex; compatibility with current membership; severity of problematic condition; and other considerations such as motivation to attend and agency priorities. When members were accepted for the group, respondents viewed attendance as voluntary in slightly over half of the groups, required in 26%, and a mixture in 21%.

Group Arrangements

Group meetings varied from once a week in 44% of the groups, the most typical pattern, to no established pattern in one group. The remaining groups met anywhere from every day to less than once a month. The length of meetings showed little variation from usual group practice. In half of the groups, the meetings were one hour or less; most of the rest met for between 61 minutes and two hours.

The overwhelming majority (77%) of these groups had been in existence for two years or more. Only 9% of the groups had met for less than a year. In 55% of the groups, members were asked to make a commitment to attend for either a specific number of sessions (ranging from 1 to 24 meetings) or for all of the sessions offered while they were identified clients or during their residence in an inpatient facility. In groups requiring no commitment, attendance appeared to be based solely on member need and motivation.

For the 35 groups in which an average attendance rate could be identified, there was wide variation in the typical number of sessions attended. In many (71 %) of these groups, membership was relatively short-term, with estimates of average attendance ranging from one to ten sessions. In less than a third (29%) of these groups, membership tended to be longer-term and average attendance ranged from eleven to fifty sessions. For the other 31 groups in the sample, no standard pattern of attendance could be identified.

Entry Patterns

The theme of variation continues in the patterns of member entry reported for our sample of open-ended groups. Members were added almost every meeting in 29% of the groups, every two to four meetings in 20%, every five to ten meetings in 18%, and at intervals greater than ten meetings for 5%. For 29% of the groups, the timing of member additions was variable within each of the groups. The number of members added at one time was predominantly one (41%) or two (24%). In an additional 5% of the groups, either 4, 5, or 14 members were typically added at one time. About one-third of the groups had developed no pattern for the number of member additions.

Exit Patterns

Exit patterns for members of the open-ended groups studied are even more variable than those related to entry. In 38% of the groups there was no pattern related to how often members left. In the remaining groups, members left almost every meeting in 20% of the groups, every two to four meetings in 20%, every five to ten in 20%, and only after more than ten meetings in 2%. The number of members leaving at one time was not predictable in 41% of the groups, was reported as one member in 42%, two members in 16%, and three members in 2% of the groups.

Procedures for Entry

Given the potential for disruption created by members entering the groups in the sample in an often unpredictable fashion, it is not surprising that all but two of the groups (97%) had procedures for handling member entry. Response to a checklist of possible procedures indicated that in 62% of the groups employing procedures, pre-group interviews were used, 89% of the groups had verbal orientation, 27% used structured exercises and activities, and 12% used other introductory mechanisms like taking a group pledge. Procedures were most often used in combination, with two-thirds of the groups using two or more of these procedures.

In slightly more than two-thirds of the groups, the group members were involved with the worker in orienting new members. In the remaining groups, workers took total responsibility for this task and occasionally involved other personnel. The most common means of orienting new members was the presentation of group purposes; this occurred in almost all of the groups (98%). Introduction of new members (91%) and the presentation of rules or norms (84%) were also very frequent approaches and over half (56%) included presentation of member responsibilities. Further, in 20% of the groups other means were used such as previewing the group or reviewing group history. Usually more than one approach was taken to orientation; four-fifths of the groups reporting their approach to orientation used three or more of the five means cited. Only two groups used one means alone.

Procedures for Termination

In contrast to the pervasive use of entry procedures by almost all of the sample, somewhat fewer groups reported established procedures to deal with member termination: 71% had procedures while 29% reported no procedures. Responses to a checklist of possible exit procedures indicate that group discussion related to termination issues and evaluation was a procedure used in most of the groups (91%). Structured exercises or activities (32%), post-group interviews (23%), and other procedures (28%) such as provision of refreshments were used less frequently. In slightly less than one-half of the groups only one procedure was used, while a combination of procedures was employed in the other groups.

As with entry, responsibility for handling termination was most commonly shared by workers and members (72%). In some groups (23%) the workers handled termination alone, and there was one instance reported of members taking sole responsibility for termination and one group where responsibility was carried by other personnel outside the group.

All of the groups reporting termination procedures included review of achievements and expression of feelings as means to deal with member departure. Most groups also discussed members' future plans (94%), and a number of groups (32%) had additional means of dealing with members leaving, such as requiring advance notice of member departure or focusing on unfinished business. Multiple means were uniformly used to deal with termination.

Discussion

The large number of open-ended groups located in a small geographic area indicates that open membership is becoming a relatively common feature of groups designed by seasoned practitioners. A majority of these open-ended groups appear to be an established and accepted part of agency services and do not represent an experimental venture. It should be noted that our sample of open-ended groups was provided by practitioners with professional education in social work, experience, and considerable training in group approaches. These social workers have adapted their knowledge and skills in a way that facilitates responsive service delivery in a wide range of settings. The open-ended groups they have created provide ongoing service to adults, adolescents and children with needs related to mental health, aging, family and interpersonal relations, and health.

Despite the varied client populations served, these groups held many purposes in common and typically were designed to meet a multiplicity of needs, an indicator of their versatility and flexibility. They tended to meet on a regular basis and to share common group experiences stemming from the unpredictability and disruption associated with open membership. While there was considerable range in the number of sessions attended, the predominant mode was short-term attendance. Given the uncertain and brief nature of membership, workers may find it helpful to have a number of purposes available so that they can be responsive to those present and quickly focus their work together. The groups in our sample did exhibit a variety of patterns. They differed in size, frequency of meetings, requirements of attendance, criteria for membership, source of members, as well as the frequency and amount of membership change.

The primary identifying characteristic of open-ended groups is that of membership change: over time, old members depart and new members are added, sometimes in the same session. Because turnover was fairly frequent in the groups in the sample, entry and exit were common themes. While the number of individuals involved in membership change was typically small, entry and exit still constitute disruption of group activities. Just as constant turnover affects a group and its members, groups that experience continuity for longer periods may react even more strongly to the introduction of a new member or loss of an old. These groups may have had more opportunity to develop cohesion and lower expectations for change in membership.

In many of the groups there was a certain degree of unpredictability related to the arrival of new members and the departure of old. A sizeable minority of the groups studied had no definable pattern related to the timing of membership changes. Further, since only slightly more than half of the groups had requirements for attendance, practitioners often were unaware of how many members would be present at any given session. Thus, changes in membership disrupting the flow of group life and some unpredictability are expected features in these open-ended groups.

Established procedures for orienting new members and handling termination of members who are leaving can minimize potential disruption to the group and offset unpredictability. This is especially critical since members of open-ended groups often attend for only a short time. Almost all of the groups had procedures related to member entry and almost three-fourths had a standard approach for dealing with termination. Perhaps termination procedures were less developed because members often left without advance notice. Workers and members may have had no further contact with them. In contrast, new arrivals had to be oriented whether or not they were anticipated.

Although procedures for termination are not used as frequently as those for entry, their development merits consideration. Old members need to express feelings related to loss, envy, abandonment, or pride in others' accomplishments, to facilitate reintegration as they proceed with their work together. Even when members are only in the group for a brief period, there should be an opportunity to reflect on the experience and to evaluate its impact. Further, when turnover is rapid, termination routines can give a sense of stability to the group. Termination procedures have a way of signaling to the remaining members that each individual is important to the group's life and will be missed on departure, reinforcing the importance of the group. Even members who do not return to the group for termination may be contacted, in person, by phone, or in writing, to review their time with the group.

Workers and members most often shared responsibility for entry and exit routines. While group workers strive to have members take responsibility for group functioning, there may not be sufficient time for leadership to emerge in groups where members come for brief periods. Thus, it may be necessary for the worker to assume some leadership role in entry and exit, involving the members as much as possible. Practitioners used a variety of approaches to orient new members and speed integration, including both discussion and structured activities. They described a number of innovative techniques for connecting new members to old and providing continuity to group purposes and traditions. Many of the rituals were designed to convey information about the group and the potential help it could offer. New members were sometimes given a written description, allowed to preview sessions on video tape or as observers, greeted with songs or welcome cards, offered refreshments or assigned a "buddy." Old members often reviewed their goals and needs and assisted newcomers in defining their stake in the group. These varied traditions not only help integrate new members into the group system, but also ease tension for the rest of the group by providing a structured way to deal with an ever-changing situation. The reaffirmation of goals, norms, and mutual interests that are a product of these procedures can be a renewing force. Since these procedures typically are routinized, the group can move quickly through the necessary beginning tasks, minimizing the boredom that might result from frequent repetition.

Even though entry tended to be handled in a more systematic way than termination, provision was made in a large number of the groups for departing members to examine and consolidate their group experience and for the remaining members to reassess and continue with their work together. Discussion may include reminiscence, evaluation of progress, exploration of future plans and available support systems, and expressions of loss. When termination was anticipated, many groups had some special way of wishing departing members well and celebrating their gains, sometimes through tangible means such as parties, cards, remembrance booklets, legacy tapes, and awards. In one children's group, members previewed each member's departure in a symbolic train ride; and, several groups indicated that ritual activities and discussions were conducted with those remaining even when members had departed unexpectedly. In a number of cases, open membership implied ongoing availability of group support and when this was true, members who left were encouraged to return if they wished.

The procedures used to cope with entry and exit in this sample of open-ended groups tend to reinforce the value of the group and promote stability despite frequent change. Workers may not be able to anticipate new arrivals or sudden departures, but routine responses to these events can reduce the uncertainty of open membership and allay the negative impact of change. We would recommend that every group develop systematic procedures for dealing with member entry and departure. These procedures should address not only the needs of new arrivals and members who are leaving but should also encompass the group's need to reintegrate after every membership change.

Practitioners responding to our questionnaire have developed a broad array of means for dealing with the disruptive effect of membership turnover despite a lack of theoretical and practice guidelines. They cope creatively with constant change, using entry and exit rituals to ease the work of the group as members enter and leave. Their responses represent practice adaptations of theory pertaining to closed groups.

The time-limited membership often characteristic of open-ended groups must be considered in both group composition and orientation. In the majority of groups in the sample, some type of inclusion or exclusion criteria were used to recruit and select members with common interests, a practice which should expedite rapid group formation and effective group functioning. The fact that membership was regarded as completely voluntary in over half of the groups and partially voluntary in an additional one-fifth may reflect the workers' recognition that members must be motivated to accomplish their goals in a limited period of time. Furthermore, the requirement that members commit themselves to attendance for a prescribed number of sessions in slightly over half of the groups may speak to the attempt to bring some stability and predictability to a group situation constantly in flux.

Working with open-ended groups demands a high level of skill, knowledge, and flexibility. To achieve the purposes for which their groups are formed, practitioners must continually and instantly assess individual and group behavior and respond to ever-changing situations. They must be ready to alter plans to accommodate to unanticipated membership turnover or unforeseen crises. They must be skilled in a variety of approaches so that they can be responsive to the members present at any particular session. They must be able to foster the rapid development of relationships which facilitate the achievement of members' goals. Sometimes, workers may need to be directive to keep groups moving, to fill vacuums created by membership loss, and to ensure that group purposes and maintenance needs are given adequate attention; at other times, when members are able to perform leadership functions, the worker must be prepared to take a less active role.

These practitioners must also fend off the tedium that comes with constant repetition. Since members come for limited periods, entry and exit must be encountered over and over, creating the potential for worker boredom and burnout. Additionally, group workers may be involved in training students and other co-workers in the open ended approach. These taxing leadership demands may explain, to some extent, why the vast majority of open-ended groups are served by two or more co-leaders. Co-leadership is one way to secure support and cope with the difficulties and frustrations these groups may entail.

Since new members continually enter open-ended groups and old members depart, the formation and termination phases of group development are perpetually repeated, even if only for a brief period each time. When members remain in groups for longer intervals, the initial or formative phase of development may occur through a gradual build-up to the next phase; in the time-limited atmosphere of the open-ended group this process must be telescoped. Similarly, as termination occurs frequently, and sometimes without warning, leaders must be prepared to adapt their knowledge of termination guidelines to take account of members' often brief stays and the group's need to proceed with its work.

Our preliminary analysis of this sample of 66 open-ended groups suggests that open membership has become a standard feature of group services. Most of the groups in our sample had been in operation for several years, a testament to their ability to attract members on a continuing basis. The procedures practitioners have developed tend to maintain group stability and integration in the face of unpredictable and sometimes disruptive membership change. While we do not have any evidence indicating that these groups accomplish all the purposes they pursue, we have data which suggest many groups move beyond the initial stages of group development. Further, the longevity of these groups and the statements of our respondents affirm the importance of open-ended groups in meeting members' needs.

The frequent use of open-ended groups by trained and skilled practitioners warrants further examination and research. Open membership deserves increased conceptual attention. Practitioners who are demonstrating the utility and flexibility of open-ended groups in a variety of settings offer an ample data base for describing critical features of this approach and for developing theory to guide intervention.

Editors' Note. This paper was originally presented at the 5th Annual Symposium for the Advancement of Social Work with Groups, in Detroit, MI, October 21, 1983; and published in 1985 by Haworth Press as *Time as a Factor in Group Work, a special issue of Social Work with Groups*. (Galinsky, M. J. and Schopler, J. H., (1985). *Social Work with Groups*, 8(2), 67-80. DOI: 10.1300/J009v08n02_07.) Reprinted by permission of Taylor & Francis Ltd, http://www.tandfonline.com.

Reference

Schopler, J. H. & Galinsky, M. J. (1984). Meeting practice needs: Conceptualizing the open-ended group. *Social Work with Groups*, 7 (Summer), 3-21.

Groupwork as the Georgian Association of Social Workers' Approach for Promoting Collective Action

Natia Partskhaladze

Introduction by Mark Doel

The North Carolina IASWG Symposium saw the inauguration of the Association's International Scholar. For some time, IASWG has had an aspiration to sponsor a scholar of international standing coming from outside the Association and from a part of the world where we do not, as yet, have a local organization (a Chapter). It was with great pleasure, then, that we invited Dr. Natia Partskhaladze as our first International Scholar to give the Sumner Gil Memorial Plenary Presentation. Dr. Partskhaladze was one of the very first Georgians to achieve a Masters in Social Work (from George Warren Brown School of Social Work at Washington University in St. Louis, USA) and to return to Georgia to be a founding member of the group of social workers and academics who established social work education in the former Soviet republic of Georgia in the years after 2005.

Georgia is a very old country, with a language that was codified as far back as the fifth century. It lies in the Caucasus, with Russia to the northeast and Turkey to the southwest. Georgia restored its independence from the Russian Empire in 1918, but its social democratic government lasted a mere three years. It was occupied by Bolshevik Russia in 1921, then incorporated into the Soviet Union a decade later. In 1991 Georgia regained independence, following the disintegration of the USSR. Not until the "Rose Revolution" of 2003 did the country achieve a degree of stability and economic progress, and the circumstances became ripe for the introduction of social work education (Doel *et al* 2016; Kachkachishvili, 2014).

"Social work activities" were undertaken in Georgia before "social work" was recognized with the introduction of BSW and MSW education and training at Iv. Javakhishvili Tbilisi State University. Groupwork, too, is congruent with the family-oriented, traditional community-based life in Georgia. Individualism was much restricted in Soviet Georgia, and the experience of forced collectivization under the Soviet authorities followed by the introduction of free market economic and social policies after independence in 1991, have perhaps induced a certain ambivalence with regards to 'groupwork'. As groupworkers, we know the power of groups and, whilst striving for positive mutual aid in groups, we also know that "groupthink" can lead to destructive and oppressive environments (Janis, 1972; Turner and Pratkanis,1998).

A striking example of groupwork is to be found in the collective action taken by the early group of Georgian qualified social workers who inaugurated social work in Georgia and founded the Georgian Association of Social Workers (GASW) in 2004. Their work is an inspiration for groupworkers around the globe. When Dr. Partskhaladze concluded her presentation, one of the delegates was heard to say, "I feel like we have been listening to the Georgian Jane Addams", to which I was able to reply, "Except that here we have *a group* of Jane Addamses!"

Groupwork as the Georgian Association of Social Workers' Approach for Promoting Collective Action

Natia Partskhaladze

It is an honor and a pleasure to present a keynote at the 37th Annual Symposium of the International Association for Social Work with Groups. It is a great opportunity to share with the audience the work that the Georgian Association of Social Workers is doing in Georgia, an example of a less formal, less structured way of doing group work; and for me to learn from experts in group work about its conventional, more professional dimensions. I would like to express my appreciation to Professor Mark Doel for suggesting this invitation to the Symposium as a representative from Georgia. This suggestion can be explained by his extensive knowledge of Georgian culture and traditions, as well as a history of social work development in the country.

Background to Social Work in Georgia

Georgia is a homeland for up to four million people and is located on the Black Sea coast, along the Greater Caucasus Mountains, at the crossroads of Europe and Asia. The land of Georgia has been inhabited for about two million years. Complete skulls of adult human beings dating back 1.8 million years were recently found not far from Tbilisi, the capital of Georgia, and they are believed to belong to the human beings who were among the first to leave Africa and colonize the rest of the world.

The history of the country of Georgia spans more than 2500 years. Georgian is one of the oldest living languages in the world and has its own distinctive alphabet which is one of the 14 existing alphabets globally. Georgia (the Kingdom of Iberia) adopted Christianity in the early 4th century and the first Georgian Cross – Saint Nino's Cross – was made of the two pieces of grapevines. This demonstrates the importance given to wine culture in Georgia.

Several countries in the Caucasus region are competing for the title of the birthplace of wine, though recently the European Union has awarded Georgia the exclusive right to sell wine with the slogan "Georgia – the Cradle of Wine." Wine has always been a source of strength in local Georgian society. Winemaking and wine drinking, tied up with Georgian feasting and toast making, are integral parts of Georgian culture. The Georgian *supra* (feast) is a way of socializing with friends and family and is headed by a *Tamada* – a toastmaster, who leads formal and informal gatherings. It can be argued that good Tamadas are the most experienced and effective group work facilitators in Georgia, applying their group facilitation skills for centuries!

During its long history, including 70 years of Soviet history, Georgia has been fighting to preserve the country's identity and independence. It is believed that its own language and alphabet, religion, winemaking, and other traditions have helped Georgians to maintain their national identity. The acute need to preserve independence, and hence a need for collective security, explains Georgia's traditional collectivist culture, with individuals tightly linked to their nuclear and extended families and other informal groups.

Belonging to groups is a fundamental part of the social life in Georgia. Individuals are tightly linked with their in-groups, which protect them all through their life-span, providing room for mutual support and for achieving common aims. Even so, if asked, Georgians very rarely would identify themselves as part of a group. If, however, they were introduced to the definition of a group as outlined at the European Seminar on the General Principles of Social Group Work (European Seminar, 1959; Doel, 2012), almost every citizen of the country would subscribe to being part of a group. For example, they would agree that they:

* Have close emotional ties with the group members;
* Feel a sense of belonging to the group;
* Feel accepted by other members of the group;
* Have certain responsibilities towards the group and the group members; (which we might now call mutual aims and mutual aid);
* Feel loyalty towards the group.

And yet, the oppressive collective system widespread during the

Soviet years has brought negative connotation and resistance to the notion of formal groups and work done in formal groupings. The phenomenon of "social loafing," in which individuals exercise less effort to achieve a goal when they work in a group than when working alone, was particularly widespread during the Soviet era and continued after its collapse. Work in formal versus informal groups was and still can be seen as prescribed and involuntary and often lacks the characteristics of healthy, functional group work.

The last two decades after the collapse of the Soviet Union brought signs of a paradigm shift from a collectivist, towards a more individualistic culture. However, increasing desires to exercise personal freedom and individualistic global trends have not diminished the importance of group and family belonging in Georgia. The majority of families in the country still live in multigenerational households, and older persons are taken care of by the families in their homes. Relying on family members is not seen as shameful, and people reach out for informal support before approaching formal structures.

This situation is not unique for Georgia and is typical of many collectivist cultures that are experiencing transitions. It creates a specific context for the work of professionals, including social workers, group workers, and others. It requires thoughtful planning of work methods, taking into account modern developments as well as building on local traditions. This is why it is of a particular interest for me to be part of a discourse fostered by the IASWG, in which some members suggest that we be alert to group work as an everyday occurrence, taking place around us all the time and benefiting the wider public, not just specially selected "group members."

The Georgian Association of Social Workers' Approach for Promoting Collective Action

With this background in mind, let us present the process of development of the field of social work in Georgia. Just 15 years ago, social work did not exist in the country as a profession. On the one hand, the Soviet government believed that Soviet people did not have social problems, hence there was no need to develop a social work profession; and on the other hand, informal support systems were quite strong in the country and were partially making up for the lack of professional support.

In 2002, the first two U.S. educated social workers, one of whom was me, returned to Georgia after completing graduate studies there. A scholarship was provided by the Open Society Institute/Soros Foundation to one or two professionals with an academic qualification in related fields and/or related working experience to study social work in the United States at Washington University, St. Louis or Columbia University, New York. Every year the group was joined by additional graduates and in 2004, six of these graduates established the first and only professional association of social workers in Georgia. In 2014, GASW united up to 600 members, which is a substantial number for a small country with a short history of social work. GASW is considered an important player in the field of social work, not only in Georgia but many other countries of Eastern Europe and Central Asia.

Understanding more about group work has led me to an understanding of the establishment and development of GASW as an example of group work at a macro level. When studying at the George Warren Brown School of Social Work and working in different social services in St. Louis, Missouri, I knew that after returning home I would not have an opportunity to join existing services, as there were almost none. During the first years of the Program, my colleagues returned home to Georgia with exactly the same understanding; we were "all in the same boat." Each of us was eager to support the development of social work profession in Georgia and saw a need to join forces and establish a group – now called GASW.

GASW fulfilled all five of the criteria of a group advanced earlier in this presentation – a mutual aim; trust and respect in each other; emotional ties; a feeling of belonging and loyalty to the group; and in the case of GASW, we were prepared to develop a structure (a non-governmental organization) with a clear division of tasks and responsibilities.

The group has elected a chairperson responsible for managing and facilitating the group work. GASW has introduced three- to six-year terms, and I am the third chairperson (leader) of the Association. GASW is acknowledged as an important player in Georgian social work and has facilitated many important developments in the field of social work, independently or in collaboration with others. Some of the key developments include:

- Establishing social work academic programs in the country (made possible with valued support from Professor Doel, his colleagues at Sheffield Hallam University, and other partners). Most of GASW's founders continue to teach in those programs;
- Developing and running the field education component of social work curricula, including training of field educators and providing ongoing support to the groups of students;
- Contributing to major reforms in child care and other systems in Georgia that require social work and social service development;
- Developing the capacity of social services providers, including grassroots organizations in the regions of Georgia.

During the years of ongoing work as a small and now a larger group, the founders of the GASW have always demonstrated loyalty and commitment to the common aim, as opposed to the individual interests and needs of the leaders of the group. Now that I analyze the work of our organization as an example of group work, I believe that having support from an external professional group facilitator would have helped our group to function even more effectively. For specialists in group work, it might be useful to further conceptualize their possible role with similar groups and teams, as it will benefit these groups, the group work concept, and the outcomes of group work in general.

As I mentioned earlier, I do not see myself as an expert in social work with groups and do not seek to convince my audience in widening the definition and scope of group work. Even though I sympathize with the approach of extending the boundaries of group work and having this method applied by specialists as well as non-specialists, I can also understand those professionals who wish to maintain boundaries of group work as a specialization and to advocate for professional training for group workers. In Georgia, which is at an early stage in the development of the social work profession, social work professionals found themselves facing similar challenges and trying to build "boundaries" for the profession. GASW leaders and many other professional social workers argue than not everyone with a kind heart and desire to help can be considered a social worker, and that academic training – and at a later stage, licensing – are required steps for practicing social work.

During the last 10 years, GASW has developed into a stable group, engaged in various activities, some of which can be also be considered as group work at different levels. The next level of GASW's group work is work with diverse population groups. GASW has conducted group work with children who were deinstitutionalized from large-scale residential settings; with internally displaced Georgian populations that fled their villages after the 2008 military conflicts; and with ethnic and religious minority women from the remote region bordering with Chechnya (Russia).

Social work with groups of Kist and Chechen women was particularly interesting. GASW worked with three self-organized groups of women, based on their common aim of establishing different community-based services: namely services for children with disabilities; older persons; and children deprived of parental care. The characteristics of the members of the group were unique and new for GASW – they were women of all ages, who mostly had limited education and restricted social roles outside of their family environments. They came from traditional, matriarchal, hierarchical communities that were not very well integrated into mainstream Georgian society. Building trust and demonstrating respect, empowering the members of the groups, strengthening their self-confidence and knowledge, and defining their roles were tasks requiring professional skills and cultural sensitivity from the GASW group facilitators.

GASW is a group member of several national and international networks and plays an active role in group dynamics. The Association is a board member of the National Coalition on Child and Youth Welfare, a group of likeminded NGOs actively engaged in reforming the child care system and working on deinstitutionalization in Georgia. The group work specific to this context is much different and is built on mutual aid principles. Skills of working in such groups and especially facilitating them are neither inherited nor taught to everyone. Social workers, with their group work skills, were instrumental in supporting such group work.

Yet another level of work with groups is GASW's work with high-level government departments and international organizations. GASW is a member of groups aiming to advance child care, juvenile justice, and other system reform in the country and often facilitates the meeting sessions. In these groups GASW's role is to advocate with the government and donor agencies and convince them of the need to strengthen social work and social services. The power dynamics of similar groups, where it is important to navigate politically charged environments, to be proactive and critical, and at the same time to maintain the government's trust and acceptance, is an environment where social workers' professional methods and skills are certainly significant.

With these examples I conclude my presentation about the context of group work in Georgia alongside the internal and external work of GASW, seen through the group work lens. GASW chairperson and leaders acknowledge that GASW has much to learn from the International Association for Social Work with Groups and from the group work gurus present at the event. It is my hope that participation in this symposium will be a first step towards an effective collaboration between GASW and IASWG. GASW would be happy to contribute to thinking on how to strengthen group work through academic education and training in countries like Georgia where mutual aid is well-established, yet the recognition of formal group work might still be lacking.

The Georgian *Tamada*, who leads the toasts and the process at Georgian *Supra* **(festivals) is the ultimate Group Facilitator**; Courtesy, Mark Doel

GASW

ႱႠႵႠႰႧႥႤႪႭႱ ႱႭႺႨႠႪႳႰ ႫႳႸႠႩႧႠ ႠႱႭႺႨႠႺႨႠ
GEORGIAN ASSOCIATION OF SOCIAL WORKERS

Banner for the Georgian Association of Social Workers (GASW)

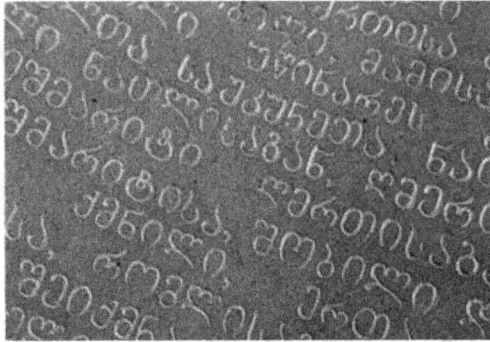

Georgian script, unique to the Georgian language

Georgia lies in the Caucasus

The Georgian Orthodox Church and the oldest viticulture in the world are both deeply embedded in Georgian culture

References

Doel, M. (2012). 'When is a group not a group? In G. Tully, K. Sweeney, & S. Palombo (Eds.), *Groups: Gateways to Growth – Proceedings of the 19th International Symposium on Social Work with Groups* (pp. 129-38). London: Whiting & Birch.

Doel, M., Kachkachishvili, I., Lucas, J., Namicheishvili, S.& Partskhaladze, N. (2016). Creating social work education in the Republic of Georgia. In I. Taylor, M. Bogo, M. Lefevre & B. Teater (Eds.), *International Handbook of Social Work Education* (pp 96-106). London: Routledge.

European Seminar on the General Principles of Social Group Work, (1959). Report of the European Seminar on the principles and practice of group work, Sèvres, Paris. Geneva: Technical Assistance Office of the United Nations.

Kachkachishvili, I. (2014). Postmodern condition" of internal politics in Georgia. In *Armenia and Georgia in the Context of Current Political Developments, New Challenges and Opportunities in the Realm of Regional Security: Proceedings of the Armenian, Georgian Expert Forum* (pp. 39-42). Tbilisi, Georgia: Friedrich Ebert Foundation.

Janis, I. (1972), *Victims of groupthink*. Boston: Houghton Mifflin.

Turner, M. & Pratkanis, A., (1998), Twenty five years of groupthink research. *Organizational Behavior and Human Decision Processes 73*(2), 105–115.

Actualizing the Global Agenda for Social Work and Social Development through Social Group Work

Carol S. Cohen, Alexis Howard, Kyle McGee, and Erin Nau

Abstract: When skillfully implemented across organizational levels, group work approaches appear highly effective in making progress towards achieving the Global Agenda for Social Work and Social Development (IASSW, IFSW, ICSW, 2012) Four exemplary cases studies of diverse programs in the Metropolitan New York area demonstrate group work integration at the client, staff and administrative levels. Thematic analysis suggests that knowledge and commitment to group work supports cross sector infusion of nimble, cultural relevant, and social justice informed practices that contribute to program effectiveness, staff development, and client and community benefit.

Introduction

The *Global Agenda for Social Work and Social Development: Commitment to Action* (IASSW, IFSW, ICSW, 2012) was developed and ratified by three international organizations in areas of social work education, practice, and policy. The International Association of Schools of Social Work, International Federation of Social Workers, and International Consortium for Social Welfare pledged that they and additional signatories will address four key objectives and areas of action of the *Global Agenda*: "Promoting social and economic equalities; promoting the dignity and worth of peoples; working towards environmental and community sustainability; and strengthening recognition of the importance of human relationships" (IASSW et al, 2012, p.1).

The *Global Agenda* appears unique in that it calls for these objectives to be concurrently pursued on all organizational levels, including management, supervision, and direct engagement with clients, service users, staff, and community members. Most strikingly, the *Global Agenda* pledges that the original framers and other adopting organizations must first look at their own organizational practices and work to insure that operations of large scale groups (such as the International Association for Social Work with Groups) correspond with the four key objectives of the *Global Agenda*. This can be seen as an example of Middleman and Wood's "self" principle – "Take everything you know and apply it to yourself" – scaled up to include group, organizational, and community levels (1990, p.67).

The International Association for Social Work with Groups (IASWG) shares the goals of the *Global Agenda* for a socially and economically just, sustainable world that promotes the potential of relationships to insure human rights and the dignity of all people. Beyond its similar aspirations, IASWG offers a key perspective to achieving the *Global Agenda* – the belief that social group work and team-based approaches are essential throughout human service organizations. As expressed in the IASWG mission statement:

> Within this group work context, we believe in the value and importance of diversity to enrich and strengthen our work and its relevance in the broad social environment. We affirm that we aspire to provide equitable opportunities for participation for all members, and that all aspects of the organization will be characterized by respect for, inclusion, and representation of people across all aspects of social identity (IASWG, 2018).

This paper, developed from a workshop session at the 2015 IASWG Symposium, uses a multiple case study approach to understand how social group work and related team approaches are integrated in exemplary human service programs to facilitate the wellbeing of clients and communities. Each of the four case studies describes how the organization promotes an objective of the *Global Agenda* and how it uses group methods throughout the organization, including the community and client level, the staff and middle management level, and the upper management and administrative level. Before presenting the case studies, we discuss the relevant literature on group work in organizations, describe our process of developing this project, and report on the methods used to identify cases and to collect and analyze information. Following the case study reports, we elaborate on themes emerging from our analysis of the group work approaches of these organizations, and we describe our activities and plans to expand this project.

Group Work across Organizational Levels

Much of the literature on literature on group work in organizations supports group work practice at the grassroots or client and community level (East, Manning & Parsons, 2011; Maidment & Brook, 2014; Staples, 2012; Tropman, 2004). There are few empirical studies, however, that examine group work knowledge, competencies, and skills through multiple levels of organizations (Cohen & Tully, 2014). Contextual conditions such as organizational culture and organizational climate (Glisson, 2007; Griffin & Mathieu, 1997) may influence the use of group and teamwork practices in daily operations. Literature discussing groups on the middle/staff and upper/management levels is found in several scholarly domains, including workforce development (Tully, 2009) organizational theory and industrial psychology (Griffin & Mathieu, 1997; Sundstorm, McIntyre & Halfhill, 2000), and business management (Hodson, 2010; Yang & Guy, 2011).

Despite the various perspectives on the influence and goals of group work within organizational life, there is some consensus that the middle level (called "group" level) of staff activity is a critical organizational subsystem (Burke, 2011). This is the level where staff members engage in the relational aspects of the work, share responsibilities, and experience a sense of interdependence and collaboration (Sundstrom, McIntyre, Halfhill and Richards, 2000). Research suggests that significant changes in organizational practices and procedures are possible through the activities at this subsystem level (Burke, 2011), which raises questions about how these influences can be enhanced when group work is supported and integrated across all levels of the organization.

Group work in organizations is a dynamic, complex, and multidimensional phenomenon (Ilgen, Hollenbeck, Johnson & Jundt, 2005). Group-focused skills can impact teams as well as the relationships and social interactions between and among work groups (Totterdell, Wall, Holam, Diamond & Epitropaki, 2004). In their efforts to promote effectiveness, organizations increasingly look to the benefits of group work to yield improved work outcomes (Yang & Guy, 2011). Walter and Bruch (2008) observed the benefits of teams, including enhanced collective task performance, decreased absenteeism, and overall workforce wellness. For workforce members in multi-level organizational environments, the inherent intimacy of group membership becomes significant for daily interactions and for peer support (Vandyke, Knippenberg, Kerschreiter, Hertel & Wieseke, 2007), especially in highly stressful environments.

Within recent decades, work groups in organizations have emerged as places where staff members are able to participate in interdependent decision-making (Sundstrom, McIntrye, Halfhill & Richards, 2000). Collective decision-making becomes particularly empowering in larger organizational structures such as complex bureaucracies, as illustrated in the innovative casework practice of "teaming" (OCFS, 2010) in child welfare practice. Teaming enhances traditional case management practices through group supervision and insures that decisions surrounding incidents of child maltreatment no longer rest on individual workers, but rather on the entire team, thereby easing individualized stress and blame (Hodson, 2000; OCFS, 2010).

Shifts from individual knowledge and direction to collective knowledge and action may ultimately lead to group and organizational empowerment (Gutierrez, GlenMaye & DeLois, 1995). As industries flatten their hierarchal structures, groups and teams promote the exchange of learning across organizations (Griffin & Mathieu, 1997; Van Dick, et al., 2007). Group work may improve job satisfaction (Van Dick et al., 2007; Yang & Guy, 2011) and increase organizational capacities to serve clients and communities in their quest for empowerment, goal attainment, and hope for change (East, Manning & Parsons, 2011; IASGW, 2010).

Project Development

Our interest in this area of inquiry was sparked when two of us (Alexis Howard and Carol Cohen) attended Social Work Day at the

United Nations in March 2012, where we witnessed the Presidents of the International Association of Schools of Social Work, International Federation of Social Workers, and International Council on Social Welfare present the *Global Agenda for Social Work and Social Development* to Helen Clark, Administrator of the United Nations Development Program (2012, Social Work Day at the UN). We were inspired by the vision and objectives of the *Global Agenda*, especially the element of accountability to examine one's own organization.

The directive to implement cross-system applications of the *Global Agenda's* value-based objectives throughout human service organizations intrigued us and stimulated our thinking on how group work could be central to this effort. Seizing the moment, we invited David Jones, one of the drafters of the *Global Agenda* and past President of the International Federation of Social Workers, to meet with us and other IASWG members in New York, at Adelphi University's Manhattan Center. David Jones shared an overview of the thinking behind the development of *Global Agenda* (Jones & Truell, 2012), and we engaged in lively discussion about factors that enhanced implementation in agency practice, including the role of groups and teams. Following the meeting, we resolved to identify further links between the *Global Agenda* and group work and to develop a project to bring this intersection to IASWG and the broader social work community.

As we considered the integration of group work throughout organizations, our team (including the authors and George Getzel) began to identify human service agencies that were widely considered to be both highly effective and strongly identified with group work. Over the course of our discussions, we moved from a broad discussion of organizations to a more specific focus on exemplary organizations that intentionally integrate group methods to enhance overall service delivery. We found that programs within many of the exemplary organizations were closely aligned with at least one, and often more than one, of the four broad objectives of the *Global Agenda*. Through this process of deliberation, we outlined criteria for a multiple case study approach, focusing on exemplary organizations that operated in concert with goals of the *Global Agenda* and that integrated group approaches at three organizational levels – the service delivery or client level, the staff and middle management level, and the upper management and administrative level.

Exemplary Case Study Approach

The use of exemplary case studies crosses a number of fields of research (Evans, Harvey, & Turnbull, 2012, Fitzpatrick, 2004, Pacione, 2003). Exemplars are particular cases (human service organizations in our study) that are seen as excelling at specific tasks and that can be studied in comparison with others (Evans, Harvey, & Turnbull, 2012). The use of exemplars in a multiple case study allows for detailed reflection and comparison within a specific case or across cases (Fitzpatrick, 2004; Evans, Harvey, & Turnbull, 2012). In addition to showing different ways that organizations excel, reports of exemplary organizational strategies highlight promising ideas and encourage their potential use in practice (Pacione, 2003). We used the exemplary case study approach to examine specific organizations that seek to achieve at least one objective of the *Global Agenda* and that use group work across organizational levels.

We identified an initial pool of regional human service organizations based on their reputation in the field and their extensive use of group work in service delivery and across the organizational structure. We envisioned the project as having an international scope, but we decided to focus on regional exemplars as a preliminary step. We believed that by establishing a general protocol and presenting initial findings, we could interest other IASWG members and supporters in identifying additional exemplars in their regions and contributing to the study.

From our initial pool, we selected four regional exemplars. Each author was responsible for contacting one of the identified agencies and explaining our purpose. If the organization's director agreed, the author moved on to collecting information and constructing the case study. As part of this initial outreach, we explained that confidentiality could not be guaranteed, since the mission and structure of the organization would be difficult to disguise. In each case presented in this paper, the director agreed to have the name of the organization revealed.

It is important to identify some significant limitations to this inquiry. First, we relied on our own collective knowledge of organizations and did not conduct a broader reputational study to validate our choices. We chose organizations known for their group work approaches, and, not surprisingly, all had some connection to the International Association for Social Work with Groups. In addition, we had some previous contact or familiarity with the administrators of the organizations to which we were assigned. We focused our interviews on how the organization integrated group work approaches, which could be seen as looking for confirmation of the exemplar status. Lastly, we understood that identifying four cases within a relatively small geographic area would limit the generalizability of our findings. Further exemplary cases will be explored during the international phase of the project.

Although this study was limited to human service agencies within the New York metropolitan region, the four exemplars were diverse in size, history, programmatic components, auspices, funding structure, client populations, and community constituents. One exemplar was a sectarian/religious organization that provides nonsectarian services; three exemplars were not-for-profit agencies; and one exemplar was a large public institution. One organization was located in the Long Island suburbs; one was in Queens and one in Brooklyn; and the public agency has locations in all five boroughs of New York City.

We interviewed leaders of the exemplary organizations using a common, flexible interview guide. In addition, we referred to organizational documents and published articles. Our team consulted with each other regularly throughout the project to review progress and to address any concerns. Once we each had drafted a case study description, we identified a preliminary set of themes that might have cross-case relevancy. In preparation for our presentation in at the IASWG Symposium, we developed a set of questions for workshop participants related to themes that they saw in the exemplars. We also planned to ask participants about their own organizational experiences and their interest in joining this project in the future.

Case Study One: Center for Family Life

The Center for Family Life (CFL), a program within SCO Family of Services, is a community-based social services agency located in the Sunset Park neighborhood of Brooklyn, New York. The mission and purpose of the program is to promote social and economic equality for children, adults, and families through a comprehensive range of neighborhood-based family and social services. CFL works extensively with immigrant families, primarily from Hispanic and Caribbean countries, providing family counseling; neighborhood-based foster care; cultural, educational, and recreational programs at neighborhood public schools; adult and youth employment programs; and an emergency storefront for food and advocacy.

CFL was selected as an exemplar because of its successful grassroots efforts supporting empowerment of immigrant families, as well as its unique and comprehensive integration of group work through its entire operation. This work is closely allied with the *Global Agenda's* goal of "promoting social and economic equalities" (IASSW, IFSW, ICSW, 2012). The co-director of CFL, Julie Stein-Brockaway, is a long-time member of IASWG who has worked with her executive team to develop an organizational system that is based on a social group work approach.

Group Work on the Community/Client/Direct Services Level

The Center for Family Life integrates group work into all programs where participants receive services. A unique community program that is based on group work is the worker co-ops program. Vocational co-operatives are an effective approach to microeconomic growth within communities around the world that experience pervasive poverty and lack of resources to meet basic needs. The goals of the CFL worker co-op program is to create living wage jobs in a safe environment and to provide social supports and educational opportunities for members. The program has created eight worker co-ops that include businesses such as child and elder care, cleaning services, beauty salons, and food catering. Each co-op is operated from a group work approach.

Group Work on the Middle Management/Staff Level

Group work is evident at the staff and middle management level of CFL through its active use of democratic processes and learning communities in the supervision of workers. All staff and supervisors participate in monthly groups or "learning communities" that focus on professional development. The learning communities promote workers' ability to evaluate their performance and to infuse group work values and principles into their practice. Staff and supervisors collaboratively support the development of skills among workers that, once achieved, can lead to career advancement within the organization.

Group Work on the Executive/Management/Board Level

The executive leadership and board of CFL use group work principles, such as the values of representation, integration, and promotion of democratic group processes, throughout the agency. The Senior Round Table, a leadership group that consists of selected workers from each CFL program, helps actualize the CFL annual goals. Annual goals are generated collectively by the entire program staff in a yearly retreat, and the Senior Round Table continues to meet monthly over the course of the year to facilitate strategic planning for goal attainment. The CFL senior management and board believe that the Senior Round Table must have representation from all levels of staff to to meet programmatic goals and to realize the purpose of the organization.

Key Case Study Themes

The organizational environment of the Center for Family Life is informed by group work principles throughout levels of agency services and administration. Democratic processes and social justice approaches are evident in all community services and there is an intentional effort to help community members share power within CFL operations. Once a community co-op project is launched, the CFL staff work with participants to set up a leadership council that systematically rotates participant leaders. A norm of consensus-building is valued and encouraged in the leadership council process.

A second major theme in the CFL case study is that professional development of staff is intentionally linked to participation in group work. CFL personnel are assigned to learning communities that serve as task and support groups to promote peer innovation and leadership. Learning communities also support staff in attaining promotion and career advancement within the organization. The use of group work to promote social justice and professional development for both clients and staff is unique to the CFL organizational vision. The two themes of promoting democratic processes and professional development increase the capacity of the Center for Family Life to fulfill its stated vision for community development.

Case Study Two: North Shore Child and Family Services

The North Shore Child and Family Guidance Center, located in Roslyn Heights, New York, exemplifies the *Global Agenda's* goal of "working towards environmental and community sustainability" (IASSW, IFSW, ICSW, 2012). The North Shore Child and Family Guidance Center is dedicated to restoring and strengthening the emotional well-being of children and families through the provision of individual, group, and family services. The agency's director, Andrew Malekoff, is a long-standing IASWG member, prolific author, and editor of *Social Work with Groups*. He highlighted North Shore's work with groups and community sustainability in his article titled "Sandy and Sandy in Seven Weeks" (Malekoff, 2013), which described two traumatic events, Superstorm Sandy followed by the Sandy Hook Elementary School Shooting

The North Shore of Long Island, New York, was one of the hardest hit areas during Superstorm Sandy in 2012. However, long before the organization was directly impacted by the devastating storm, the staff had been training and preparing for different types of crises, including hurricanes. After the storm, despite dealing with storm-related crises of their own, teams of staff members were mobilized to support individuals and families in the community. These activities were critical just seven weeks after the storm, when the organization and its clients faced the secondary trauma of the shooting at Sandy Hook Elementary School in the neighboring state of Connecticut.

Group Work on the Community/Client/Direct Services Level

North Shore Child and Family Guidance Center began as a grassroots effort by parents in Nassau County to provide services to children in need of mental health services. The parents saw that there were gaps in services, and they collaborated to launch the program in 1953. Today, the agency is known for helping the community during times of crisis. For example, staff was deployed to help children and families directly impacted by the events of September 11, 2001. The services they provided were recognized and awarded a FEMA grant. Participants in the agency's post 9/11 interventions were featured in a documentary and follow-up report that was hosted by Barbara Walters (ABC News, 2012; ABC News, 2002).

After Superstorm Sandy devastated their community, social workers created groups to treat parents and children independently as they processed traumatic events. Serivces were offered in various community sites, such as firehouses and shelters. Weeks after Superstorm Sandy, the shooting at Sandy Hook Elementary School occurred re-traumatizing children and families in Long Island. Children who expressed concerns after the hurricane about their safety were again feeling unsafe. Social workers continued to work closely with children in groups to process both traumas.

Group Work on the Middle Management/Supervisory/ Staff Level

Many of the staff members who mobilized to create and facilitate support groups for the community were dealing with their own crises at home after Superstorm Sandy. Despite dealing with their own concerns, staff went to shelters the day after the storm to help others. After a debriefing about the emerging and ongoing response efforts, informal support groups were formed for staff members, where they were able to process their own traumas. The informal groups evolved into a more formal support group, Storm Survivors, where staff members provided mutual aid related to the experiences of facilitating community groups while also dealing with their own traumas and losses.

Group Work on the Administrative/Board/Management Team Level

Andrew Malekoff, the agency director, created and participated in the Storm Survivor group, and the board of directors and members of the administration were encouraged to participate as well. Superstorm Sandy impacted staff from all areas and positions in the organization, and support groups ultimately crossed all levels of agency structure from the clients to the board of directors. This group approach engaged and supported diverse constituencies as they worked through a particular time of crisis.

Key Case Study Themes

The Northshore Children and Families Guidance Center provided immediate crisis intervention for both clients and staff during a time of devastation within their community. The staff members were active in the community to help reduce long term impacts of the trauma, while informal and formal groups supported both clients and staff. The emphasis on "caring for the caregivers" through group work allowed social workers to provide the best possible care for their clients.

Case Study Three: Administration for Children's Services

The New York City Administration for Children's Services (ACS) is New York City's public child welfare agency. The mission of the agency is to ensure the safety, permanency, and well-being of New York City children and to strengthen families. The agency is committed to protecting and supporting children, youth, and families through comprehensive child welfare, juvenile justice, and early care and education services. ACS has offices throughout the five boroughs of New York City. The largest program is the Division of Child Protection, which investigates reports of suspected child maltreatment.

ACS was selected as an exemplar because it demonstrates opportunities within large governmental systems to integrate group work principles across and within divisions and to use group work in achieving organizational goals. The agency has increased its focus on achieving *Global Agenda* goal of "recognizing the importance of human relationships" (IASSW, IFSW, ICSW, 2012) by actualizing the concept of well-being for clients and workforce members.

Group Work on the Community/Client/Direct Services Level

On the client level, many families are introduced to group work principles by way of participation in the child safety conference. Families that are known to the Division of Child Protection are encouraged to participate as team members in the child safety conference. The family, as the primary group, comes together with ACS staff and community members to analyze safety concerns and to assess family strengths and supports. Using a culturally responsive approach, the child safety conference views the child within the context of family and community. Extended family members as well as traditional and non-traditional community providers join together in planning strategies to protect the child.

MSW students (who are generally experienced ACS employees) often facilitate client-level groups, including groups for youth with behavioral and emotional challenges, support groups for parents of teens, and mandated psycho-educational groups for parent/caretakers. Held at community-based locations, these groups promote mutual aid, respect, and empowerment for clients and group participation alleviates clients' sense of isolation, lowering the risk for repeat child maltreatment.

Group Work on the Middle Management/Supervisory/ Staff Level

The Child Welfare Field Education Model is an example of a group supervision model designed for agency supervisors in their capacity as field instructors of MSW students. Through the partnership with the New York Social Work Education Consortium, the New York City Schools of Social Work, and ACS, social work faculty members are hired to enhance the skill development of ACS field instructors. Grounded in the "teaming" approach to child welfare practice, field education groups support team members in solving problems and exchanging ideas.

Front-line staff who are enrolled in MSW programs have a similar supervision group that promotes professional development and peer support in learning. Through the partnership of ACS and the Social Work Education Consortium, supervision groups view child welfare practice through a critical lens and encourage macro analysis of systems and policies. Staff members, in their role as students, examine the practical application of research and theories being taught in social work education programs, and group members use the safety of the group to share their experiences as student learners.

William Fletcher, the Deputy Commissioner of the Division for Child Protection, uses a group work approach by holding brown bag staff meetings, where the executive team and frontline practitioners engage and exchange information. Team meetings provide opportunities for staff to share experiences and to discuss complex child welfare policy and practice issues. If the team decides that an issue needs closer examination, a workgroup is formed to provide additional analysis and recommendations. Although brown bag staff meetings are held at the staff/supervisory level, workgroup recommendations open communication across staff lines and influence decisions at the management/executive level.

Group Work on the Administrative/Board/Management Team Level

The ACS executive team uses group work principles in practice and models the approach for the organization. Developed in response to several high profile child fatality cases, the group work approach is used to assess family needs and to alleviate the stress experienced by staff in a crisis driven environment. Group work and team work increase cooperation and communication across and between large divisions, promote multidisciplinary child welfare practice, and instill the values associated with a caring work environment, demonstrating that group work on all levels is possible within a large bureaucratic structure.

Key Case Study Themes

Group work within ACS, a highly bureaucratic agency, is an intentional organizational intervention in which the leaders model mutual support, organizational solidarity, and collective well-being. ACS leaders ensure that groups address the impact of trauma experienced throughout the agency, from the complex trauma experienced by clients to the secondary trauma experienced by the child welfare workforce. Despite the crisis-driven pace of public child welfare, groups and work teams provide a sanctuary for the agency's community members at every organizational level.

Case Study Four: Turning Point for Women and Families

Turning Point for Women and Families is a community-based, non-profit organization in Queens, New York. Turning Point was founded by the dynamic and well-regarded leader, Robina Niaz, to meet the needs of the Muslim community through culturally resonant services. The human rights and empowerment focus of Turning Point is closely allied with the *Global Agenda* goal of "promoting the dignity and worth of peoples" (IASSW, IFSW, ICSW, 2012). The agency provides direct services for women and family members who are affected by domestic violence; youth development programs for adolescent girls; and outreach and educational programs in the local and broader community.

Group Work on the Community/Client/Direct Services Level

In the spirit of community building and mutual aid, all Turning Point participants are encouraged to attend ongoing groups and to take leadership roles within the groups and the organization. As explained by Robina Niaz, the isolation of women who have experienced domestic violence leaves them vulnerable to abuse. The cycle of shame and stigma is broken when women join groups and discover that they are not alone. Intake primarily takes place in a group, allowing group members and staff to affirm women's courage in taking the step of coming to the agency. Ongoing, open support groups engage women in examining some of their learned behaviors, including those stemming from witnessing their mothers' experience of domestic abuse.

Groups for women soon led to the development of groups for adolescent girls, initially for the daughters of clients and then for all Muslim young women who were negotiating acculturation issues and evolving identities while maintaining community ties. Youth groups for young women have sparked peer leadership training programs, programs that connect young persons with positive role models, and an annual interfaith summit for girls. The "Mecca to Manhattan – Muslim Women Moving Mountains" program demonstrates the group-based approach to helping young women find their own strength.

Group Work on the Middle Management/Supervisory/Staff Level

Turning Point for Women and Families is a relatively small organization in which staff members develop a strong sense of family and commitment. Women who join as clients are encouraged to take on peer leadership roles and often become staff members. New staff members are expected to join the women's support groups, where they learn through immersion about situations that women in the group share as well as strategies for group* facilitation. Staff members are drawn together in groups through informal, community-building activities such as sharing meals and joining in multi-family activities. The need for staff to rely on each other is considered critical in this organization, and groups create a physical and psychic "safe space" for staff and their communities.

Group Work on the Administrative/Board/Management Team Level

The Turning Point board of directors is a diverse group of people with a range of skills and experiences. Board members work together as a team in activities that range from grant writing to program development. In addition to a desire to build a sense of community in the board, Robina Niaz values the effectiveness of groups in maximizing program quality and growth.

Key Case Study Themes

At Turning Point for Women and Families, groups appear to be the intervention of first choice, and group work is seen as a survival strategy for clients, community members, staff, and members of the board. The charismatic leader of Turning Point has cultivated a group-focused, non-hierarchical approach where possible. The infusion of group work throughout the organization is promoted by top leadership, by knowledgeable colleagues within the organization, and by group work champions in the community, such as the late Catherine (Katy) Papell.

Emerging Themes and Future Plans

Our analysis of each of the four case studies yielded preliminary themes that suggest rationales and strategies for incorporating group approaches across organizational levels. In the first case study, the Center for Family Life, themes included a democratic and justice oriented approach distinguished by the principled and knowledgeable use of group methods. Power sharing by administrators and others in positions of authority was evident through group methods across organizational levels, and staff development was provided in groups where members had both investment and voice.

In the second case study, North Shore Child and Family Services, a group response to crisis situations was developed through investment in preparing for such events and through the incorporation of groups in both formal and informal aspects of organizational life. As with the Center for Family Life, groups at North Shore Child and Family Services engaged staff across levels of responsibility and areas of expertise. Group work was the "default setting" for organizational activity.

The third case study, Administration for Children's Services, demonstrated how groups may be intentionally used in large bureaucracies to respond to traumatic situations. Groups served as service delivery systems, bureaucratic buffers, and as arenas for cross-system collaboration and cultural exchange.

In the fourth case study, Turning Point for Women and Families, group work promoted by the leadership was used as an organizational survival strategy that allowed for a parallel process of empowerment practice. Groups were organized for clients and staff throughout the organization, often with an anti-hierarchical approach blending membership and facilitation.

Collectively, the four case studies suggest a number of themes that can inform organizational practice to help achieve the *Global Agenda for Social Work and Social Development*. In each case, organizational leaders had the commitment and skills to weave group work throughout their agencies. They expected groups to help the organization achieve key outcomes at every level, and groups were the primary modality for addressing needs. Group work in the case studies was culturally responsive to internal organizational diversity as well as to the complex lives of clients and their communities. Groups served as spaces where staff members and clients learned with and from one another, sought just solutions to problems, and navigated change.

Discussion among Symposium Participants

Participants at our presentation at the IASWG Symposium responded favorably to the multiple case study approach, and they agreed that the organizations selected were appropriate exemplars with links to the *Global Agenda*. Participants appreciated that the case studies followed a common structure that addressed the integration of groups through three organizational levels.

When we asked participants to identify themes in the case studies, they noted that the integration of group work throughout organizations improved effectiveness and efficiency. Although group workers often down play the efficiency factor, the use of group work as a first, preferred strategy in the case studies engaged a large number of people in common pursuits, which may have led to more powerful and sustainable interventions. The investment in group work, even when struggles emerged, led to an enduring commitment to organizational goals. Participants commended the values and skills of the organizational leaders, noting that sharing power is important, but not easy or desirable for many administrators.

The discussion of exemplary case studies led to participants' stories of less successful cases, where groups were not integrated throughout organizations or where unskilled practice resulted in demoralizing and frustrating group experiences. Competency in group work was seen as essential in organizational leadership, and participants stressed the importance of training in this area.

As we had hoped, the discussion generated participants' interest in contributing to this project. Five participants volunteered to identify exemplary case studies from other geographical regions, including three additional countries, and from other human service arenas. Since that time, we have expanded our study with additional international partners.

Conclusion

This project integrates two important imperatives in regional and international social work: the implementation of the *Global Agenda for Social Work and Social Development* (IASSW, IFSW, ICSW, 2012), and the integral nature of group work in social work education and practice. Since the adoption and presentation of the *Global Agenda* at the United Nations in 2012, the framing organizations have called for international action that makes its implementation a priority for advocacy, presentation, and publication. Through this project as well as other activities, the International Association for Social Work with Groups is demonstrating how social work with groups supports this goal.

We close this paper with our gratitude and appreciation for the accomplishments of group work visionaries at the programs we studied: Center for Family Life of SCO Family of Services, North Shore Child and Family Guidance Center, New York City Administration for Children's Services and Turning Point for Women and Families. Group work approaches can be implemented at many levels of an organization, yet it takes true leadership to insure that group work is the model of choice for client, worker, and community empowerment and for the achievement of *the Global Agenda for Social Work and Social Development*.

References

ABC News (2020). Children of 9/11. Retrieved from http://abcnews. go.com/2020/video/children-911-parents-mother-father-ten-years-later-old-age-barbara-walters-fdny-nypd-2020-14486987

ABC News (2002) Barbara Walters Grief Special DVD. New York: ABC News.

Burke, W.W. (2011). Organization *change theory and practice.* (3rd Edition). Thousand Oaks, CA: Sage Publication, Inc.

Cohen, C. S., McGee II, K., Howard, A. & Nau, E. (2015, June). *Identifying and promoting group work strategies in actualizing the Global Agenda for Social Work and Social Development.* International Symposium, International Association for Social Work with Groups, Chapel Hill, North Carolina, United States.

Cohen, C.S. & Tully, G. (2014, October). *How group work knowledge and skills inform academic and organizational leadership.* CSWE Annual Program Meeting, Tampa, FL.

East, J. F., Manning, S.S. Parsons, R.J. (2011). Social Work empowerment agenda and group work: A workshop. In S. Henry And J. East (Eds). *Social work with groups: Mining the gold.* New York, NY: Routledge.

Evans, C., Harvey, G., & Turnbull, P. (2012). When partnerships don't 'match-up': an evaluation of labour–management partnerships in the automotive components and civil aviation industries. Human Resource Management Journal, 22(1), 60- 75.

Fitzpatrick, J. L. (2004). Exemplars as case studies: Reflections on the links between theory, practice, and context. American Journal of Evaluation, 25(4), 541-559.

Glisson, C. (2007). Assessing and changing organizational culture and climate for effective services. Research in Social Work Practice, 17(6), 736-747.

Griffin, M.A., & Mathieu, J.E. (1997). Modeling organizational processes across hierarchical levels: Climate, leadership and group process in work groups. Journal of Organizational Behavior, 18, 731-744.

Gutierrez, L. GlenMaye, L., DeLois, K. (1995). The organization context of empowerment practice: Implications for social work administration. *Social Work, 40*(6), 249-258.

Hodson R. (2010). Work group effort and rewards: The roles of organizational and social power as context. *Organization Studies, 31,* 895-916.

Ilgen, D. R., Hollenbeck, J. R., Johnson. & Jundt, D. (2005). Teams in organizations: from Input-Process – Output Models to IMOI Models. *Annual Review Psychology, 56,*517–43.

IASSW, IFSW, ICSW (2012) *Global agenda for social work and social development: Commitment to action.* Retrieved from http://cdn.ifsw.org/assets/globalagenda2012.pdf

International Association for Social Work with Groups (2015). *Standards for Social Work Practice with Groups.* New York, NY. Author. Retrieved from http://www.iaswg.org/standards

International Association for Social Work with Groups (2018). *Mission Statement.* Retrieved from www.iaswg.org/mission_statement

Jones, D.N. & Truell, R. (2012) *The Global Agenda for Social Work and Social Development: A place to link together and be effective in a globalized world.* International Social Work, 55 (4). 454-472.

Kozlowski, S.W.J., & Ilgen, D.R. (2006). Enhancing the effectiveness of work group and team. *Psychological Science in the Public Interest, 7,* 77-123.

Maidment, J. & Brook, G. (2014). Teaching and learning group work using tutorial and community engagement. *Social Work with Groups, 37*(1), 73-84.

Malekoff, A. (2013). Sandy and Sandy in seven weeks: A group worker reflects. *Social Work with Groups, 36* (4), 285-291.

Middleman, R. R., & Wood, G. G. (1990). *Skills for direct practice in social work.* NY: Columbia University Press.

New York State Office of Children & Family Services. (2001). *Teaming in child welfare: A guidebook.* New York, NY. Author.

Pacione, M. (2003). Urban environmental quality and human wellbeing: A social geographical perspective. *Landscape and Urban Planning, 65*(1), 19-30.

Social Work Day at the United Nations (March, 2012). *Partnering with the United Nations:The social work and social development global agenda.* 29th Annual Social WorkDay at the United Nations, United Nations Headquarters, NY.

Staples, L. (2012). Community organizing for social justice: Grassroots groups for power. *Social Work with Groups, 35* (3), 287-296.

Sundstorm, E., McIntyre, M., Halfhill, T., & Richards, H. (2000). Work groups: From the Hawthorne studies to work teams of the 1990s and beyond. *Group dynamics: Theory, Research, and Practice, 4,* 44-67.

Totterdell, P., Wall, T., Homa, D., Diamond, H., & Epitropaki, O. (2004). Affect networks: A structural analysis of the relationships between work ties and job related affect. *Journal of Applied Psychology, 89,* 854- 867.

Tully, G. (2009). Workplace coaching. In A. Gitterman & R. Salmon (Eds). *Encyclopedia of Social Work with Groups.* 294. New York: Routledge.

Van Dick, R., Van Knippenberg, D., Knippenberg, R., Hertel, G., Wieseke, J. (2008). Interactive effects of work group and organizational identification on job satisfaction and extra-role behavior. *Journal of Vocational Behavior, 72,* 388- 399.

Walter, F., & Bruch, H. (2008). The positive group affect spiral: A dynamic model of the emergence of positive affective similarity in work groups. *Journal of Organizational Behavior, 29* (2), 239-261.

Yang, S.B., & Guy, M.E. (2011). The Effectiveness of Self-Managed Work Teams in Government Organizations. *Journal of Business & Psychology, 26,* 531-54.

On Getting Over Oneself and Creating Space for All Voices in Group Work with Adolescents

Andrew Malekoff

Abstract: As social group workers we may come to value all the trappings associated with becoming credentialed professionals, however there will always be moments in our groups when we cannot help but feeling like helpless amateurs. It is never easy to accept and hold on to these two contradictory states at the same time. Nevertheless, we must remain present and get over ourselves in order to create a space for all voices. This plenary discusses these and related ideas for hanging in there with our groups and illustrates groups that are struggling with issues including bias, bullying, grief, and trauma from individual change and social goals perspectives. Although adolescent groups are used as illustrations, the lessons herein are universal.

Get Over Yourself and Go Easy On Yourself

Having worked with adolescents for more than 40 years, I discovered early on that whatever my professional reputation and credentials, they meant little to the kids I've worked with.

The kids I work with draw their conclusions about me as they get to know me. I, in turn, draw my conclusions about them as I get to know them, despite the labels and diagnoses assigned to them.

It helps to know, up front, that one's credentials don't impress kids; and, to know that it is highly unlikely that any of our young group members will come up to us after a group meeting and say, for example, "Hey Andy, that was a really great group, I got a lot out of it." And so, if you do this work, my suggestion is to *get over yourself* and *go easy on yourself.*

A few years ago, I conducted a survey for high school students. We were trying to find out about how they viewed the future, with hope or despair. One of the open-ended items on the survey asked them to write about anything of deep concern to them, anything at all. A few of them decided to write about the survey itself. Here's what three of them said:

> *To tell you the truth, nothing at this point concerns me at all...I am unaffected by petty problems. Also, I hate surveys, but love making the results vague and inaccurate.*

> *The one concern I do have, is being administered stupid surveys by silly people....*

> *To be brutally honest, surveys like this concern me. I mean, what the hell are you trying to understand? We're teenagers – we're angst ridden, confused, worried and most importantly: curious... It's been this way in the past, and it will be this way in the future... can't you please try to understand more quietly and without wasting our time...I doubt anyone will read this anyway.*

Assuming a Stance of Uncertainty

To create space for kids' voices I have found that it helps to *assume a stance of uncertainty*. It can be difficult to work with teenagers, in particular, if we begin by coming from a position of certainty, relying exclusively on scientifically sanctioned knowledge.

To do this we need to step outside the noise, the noise inside the group and the noise inside our heads, and reach beyond what we think we already know. We need to be in the moment and become participant observers. My colleague Camille Roman (2002) illustrated this in a story from her teenage years.

Camille told a story about growing up in an economically deprived and chaotic family and how desperately she struggled as a teenager to be heard, and how no one was ever listening. During one particularly troubling and heated exchange at a holiday gathering, Camille, whose family is from Puerto Rico, remembered: "...my face apparently betrayed my fear and confusion to an elderly aunt who was secretly thought to be a witch. Tia Mercedes turned to me with her soft face and wise eyes and whispered, 'When your tongue is silent only then can you hear'" (p. 61).

Camille said, "My Tia was telling me that...something else was going on here...and if I didn't get caught up in the noise then maybe I could understand and make sense of the chaos and it would be less frightening and I would not feel so powerless" (p. 62). And so this powerful bit of homespun advice became a life lesson for Camille and one that she credits with her success as a social worker.

As a group worker, what I know is that it is often the frenetic kids' group that has more order to it, a method to the madness if you will, than the rational, tightly controlled and superficially polite business or faculty meeting that may be rife with underlying disorder in the form of political maneuvering, power struggles, and hidden agendas bubbling just beneath the surface.

Getting over myself, assuming a stance of uncertainty and keeping my tongue silent so I can hear have helped me, as a group worker, to see more clearly the logic and order of the seemingly irrational and chaotic kids' group; in contrast to the illogic of the seemingly more rational and orderly professional adult group.

A Professional Who Looks and Feels Like an Amateur

If you do this work, then you know that group work with adolescents is rarely neat or orderly or politically correct. It is more abstract than still life, more jazz than classical, and more freestyle than philharmonic; but no less a symphony. Group work with adolescents is an acquired taste. It is not for the faint-hearted.

Oftentimes when one works with adolescent groups, within view or earshot of colleagues, parents or the public, skepticism and scorn follow. My friend, the late Ralph Kolodny, told me that what was never sufficiently described in professional journals is something most group workers experience, but few discuss. What he was referring to is the constant exposure to embarrassment and loss of face.

Despite many years practicing group work, I still see myself as professional who looks and feels like an amateur. It has never been easy to hold these two contradictory beliefs at the same time.

Getting over oneself isn't such a bad thing, after all. Actually, it's a relief. It keeps me humble. It keeps me on my toes. It reminds me that I am fallible and not perfect and, that if I don't have to have all the answers, I can ask questions; which then leaves room for other voices. The biggest take-away for me is my knowing that if the only voice I hear is my own, then I am in trouble.

But, getting over oneself is harder than it sounds. For group workers it is further complicated by the fears many of us share about working with groups – fears like *losing control* of the group.

As one group worker shared, "when I'm conducting an individual interview I know where it's going and can keep track of what's happening," but in a group they seem to "take the control and it feels like I am on my motorcycle, pumping the starter to get going, and the group members are already roaring down the road."

But, for some group workers the issue of losing control is not so much about revving engines and burning rubber. The more terrifying prospect is when groups go silent, which may also feel like a loss of control.

Silence Speaks

And, since our collective focus over this long weekend is to *create space for all voices*, I ask you to consider the idea that *silence speaks* and needs space too. Proponents of mindfulness advise us to stay in the moment, to stay present, to pay attention, moment by moment, to feelings, bodily sensations and the surrounding environment, in a judgment-free way. Silence in the group presents us with the challenge of being present with our groups, and especially when there *are no words*.

As group workers, we must reconcile the high value placed in verbal product as opposed to silent moments in the group. Silence gives voice. Good music is appreciated for the spaces between the sounds – the silent intervals – as well as the sounds themselves. Composer Leopold Stokowski said, "A painter paints pictures on canvas, but musicians paint their pictures on silence" (Stokowski, n.d.). Rather than rush to fill in the silent spaces in our groups we would do well to think about the many meanings and mysteries of silence and the value of being still, being present.

In some cultures, silence represents a show of respect. For some groups it might be used as passive resistance or to conscientiously object. And, for some group members silence can offer a few welcome moments of reflection. Don't mess with silence. Silence speaks. Following is a poem I wrote that I call: *Let it Breathe, Let it Be*, that captures my sentiments about silence in the group.

Let it Breathe, Let it Be
It's freeing
It's confining
It connects
It divides
It's calming
It's maddening
It's still
It's on edge
It's tiring
It's relaxing
It dims
It glows
It's numbing
It's renewing
It's sacred
It's dull
It's bewildering
It's illuminating

It's inevitable

Silence in the group:
It's a spiritual thing

Let it breathe
Let it be

If you remember only one thing about my talk, remember this:

losing control is not where you want to get away from, it's where you want to get to. It's only when we surrender our centrality and certainty that we can truly listen and tap in to what our group members have to offer. This is where empowerment begins.

Although it's not the primary focus of my talk this morning, in my role as executive director of a large children's mental health agency, group work is my greatest ally *and* letting go helps. To be clear: my letting go of control on the job is not the same thing as ceding authority, it's about decentralizing and sharing it.

Jaguars and Bears

For example, a little more than two years ago, when Hurricane Sandy hit the east coast (Malekoff, 2014), a number of my staff members were displaced from their homes for weeks and months. Despite the widespread impact, we provided the most rapid, sustained, and extensive response to the five emergency shelters in our region. Forty staff members and interns were deployed and covered the shelters seven days a week for weeks and weeks after the storm. We were energized because we planned well.

Months before the storm, in preparation for hurricane season, our Disaster Response Team spent time planning. On all of their minds was the near-miss of Hurricane Irene one year earlier.

The team got stuck at one point in its planning, so one of the team members, not a group worker or mental health professional but someone who was active in her sons' youth sports teams, suggested that they divide into two subgroups – the *Jaguars* and the *Bears*. At her suggestion everyone agreed to research and list the characteristics of Jaguars and Bears and then decide which best suited them. Here's what they found.

Jaguars are fast, they move with lightning speed, they power through their environment with sure accuracy; they wait for the best moment to strike. They are fearless, action-oriented, and decisive.

Bears are very intelligent, curious, and have excellent memories; they use their acute sense of smell for information about the world around them. They are strong, solid, emotionally-grounded, capable of waiting it out, and process-oriented; you cannot shake them.

In the end the team discovered that there were no pure Jaguars or Bears; they were all a mix of the two and responded accordingly. But once they embraced their roles, they took them on with energy and enthusiasm which was invaluable in spawning new bears and jaguars throughout the agency.

What does any of this – jaguars and bears – have to do with group work with kids? It has everything to do with it, because the capacity for playfulness and innovation and improvisation in an organization on a macro-level, is critical to providing a hospitable environment to practicing good group work on a micro-level. Always remember that context counts.

Speaking of which, one of the things that makes social work with groups so special and what distinguishes it as a process, is its consistent pursuit of a dual vision of individual *and* social goals.

Stars of Hope

In the aftermath of Hurricane Sandy, groups of students from Long Beach Catholic created brightly-colored wooden stars of hope and placed them on utility poles and trees around the city. On the stars the kids painted hopeful messages.

Through this simple act of support the students lifted survivors' spirits. But where's the evidence of this and how do I know it? I know it because they lifted my spirits. I live in Long Beach and I evacuated my family. We were displaced for close to two months, only to return to a home in which the entire contents and structure of the first floor were destroyed.

My hometown was devastated and nearly every resident suffered extensive damage. For weeks, on the sidewalks and in the street in front of our homes were mountains of flood-destroyed property that the news media referred to as *debris*. What they called debris were our memories.

My bicycle, which I kept in the garage, was submerged in salt-water. Fortunately, I was able to salvage it. On my first bike ride around town, several months after the hurricane, I spotted the stars of hope on telephone poles and trees all around town. I stopped by each one to read them and take photos.

Some of stars said: "Our prayers are with you," "Stay Strong," "Think of the Future," "Joy," "Love," "Dream," "Hope Takes Courage," "Bruised but not Broken," "Celebrate," and "Strong Beach."

Josh Miller said that "Although disaster is by its very nature a collective event, [it is] replete with private sorrows" (Miller, 2012, p. 283). By making gentle waves, the Long Beach students helped me to feel better, more hopeful and encouraged that there would be a better day. I posted my photos of the wooden stars of hope on Facebook and Instagram to spread the good word.

Speaking of Facebook and Instagram, there is perhaps nothing more compelling in today's world than the rise of social media and its many tools that offer exciting means for connecting with others through chatting, posting, texting and sending pictures. These are spaces where kids can give voice to their ideas, opinions, likes, dislikes, hope, and fears.

However, as we know, there are those who use social media to harass, demean and humiliate. By now, we all know tragic stories about vulnerable young people who were subjected to intolerance, cruelty, and callous disregard for their online privacy; including stories about young people who felt so trapped, that they believed taking their lives was the only option when they just could not take it anymore.

"A time comes when silence is betrayal."

As important as it is for group workers to understand that silence speaks, we must also remember, as Martin Luther King reminded us, that "A time comes when silence is betrayal." And that's when we need to stand up, speak out, and get noisy.

Recently, members of a Wisconsin middle school basketball team were lauded as heroes and rightfully so. When the boys noticed some others making fun of one of their cheerleaders—a 14-year-old girl named Desiree who has Down Syndrome—they took action, walking over to the offenders and telling them to cut it out.

As one of the boys told reporters who covered the story, "They were pointing and laughing at her from the stands. It's not funny to make fun of somebody by the way they look or act." Another said, "This is not a one-time thing. You always have to stick up for kids that are bullied. It's the right thing to do." Always remember that a good group looks outward.

Another group in New York City called Teen Pact has taken steps to combat cyberbullying by producing public service announcements that are being used nationwide. One PSA depicts a boy texting an affectionate message about a classmate. His friends then pass it on and when it goes viral he becomes the target of unrelenting teasing and taunting. The PSA message is: "It's not funny anymore, don't be an accidental bully."

Bullies Move from Playground to Cyberspace

In my agency, kids as young as 12-years-old have reported receiving emotionally devastating messages on social media, messages that *demean*: "You're stupid;" *demand*: "Why are you still alive?" and *cajole*: "Why don't you kill yourself already?" (Malekoff, 2014).

Here is a typical scenario: someone "tweets" an outlandish or awkward comment intended for a select few, and then someone on the receiving end decides to torment the sender by "re-tweeting" her comment to others. The comment soon goes "viral," potentially reaching thousands, including strangers, who then ridicule the original sender with disparaging tweets of their own.

A big problem with social networking is that there is no respite, no sanctuary. Social media never sleeps; social media is 24-7-365 and it leaves kids feeling that there is no escape; not at home, not on weekends, not on vacation, no place, nowhere, not now, not tomorrow, not on Christmas, never. A vicious, personal social networking attack on a child or teenager can feel crushing, suffocating, inescapable.

In one group, 15-year-old Cary revealed that her boyfriend wanted her to pose nude while he took pictures of her with his iPhone. She refused and he broke up with her. She was confused about why he thought it would be okay for her to do that. She said she knew a few girls who did it, but that she would never do it and risk having her pictures go viral.

The group worker asked the girls if anything helped to relieve the pressure and stress of all this. Cary said that her mom was supportive, that one weekend they had a "girls' night out" where they watched a movie in bed together. "I fell asleep with my mom. I know it's corny, but it really helped to spend together time with her when I was feeling so bad."

In another group, 14-year-old Kelly reported that a longtime friend text-messaged something insulting about Kelly's physical appearance to a mutual acquaintance. The mutual acquaintance then shared the text with Kelly, who was devastated by the betrayal, leading to a breakup of their friendship. A few strokes of the keyboard and Kelly's world was turned upside down. "It felt like she stabbed me in the back," she said.

After exploring their electronic war stories in some depth the girls considered how they might protect themselves from being bullied on social media. Among the solutions discussed was for them to "deactivate" or shut down their accounts. This drew mixed reactions. Linda said, "My mother made me deactivate my Facebook account."

The group worker said, "You feel disconnected now." She nodded and Martha said, "I would rather be bothered than excluded. My dad cut me off around Christmas vacation time. It was the worst two weeks in my life. I felt *sooo* left out." To which Jackie added, "I got my phone taken away when I ran up too many minutes for texting. My mom warned me. I was so angry. My iPphone is like my lifeline."

Although, these days, cyber-bullying has taken center stage, old-fashioned bullying is still going strong; and, one of the most troubling battlefronts is bias and profiling against anyone of Middle Eastern descent.

Old-Fashioned Bullying and Profiling

During an intergenerational forum on immigration and youth, 13-year-old Muhammad worked up the courage to speak out after listening intently to others, adults and kids, tell their stories about struggling to fit in after arriving in the U.S.

Muhammad said, with a trembling voice, that there were kids in school who taunted him. "They call me *'terrorist'* because of my name." Muhammad is an Arabic name that means *praiseworthy*. But, instead of him feeling proud, Muhammad felt like an outcast.

Muhammad sat slumped in his chair and spoke softly and guardedly, but clearly and eloquently; and he was heard by the group. By the end of the day he had received so much support for having the courage to speak out and make noise about a taboo subject that he was beaming.

During lunch break, while we waited in line for Subway sandwiches and potato chips, I stood next to Muhammad and asked him how he was doing. He said, "Everybody is telling me that I speak really good. I didn't know that I could talk so good [in front of people]. Nobody ever told me that before." Muhammad left the forum feeling *praiseworthy*, a feeling befitting his name, a name that he was given at birth that he should feel proud to have.

When Words Aren't Enough

Although in the girls' group and in the immigration forum, conversation flowed freely about the influence and impact of social media, immigration, bias and profiling; another group that was addressing trauma and loss was stuck. Getting some forward movement in the way of conversation or any process was a challenge. This group was composed of pre-teen boys and girls, post 9/11. All of the members had lost their fathers in the World Trade Center. They met in one room, while their moms and siblings met in two or three other rooms elsewhere in the building (Malekoff, 2014).

After trying to get the conversation going for a few weeks, the group worker had an idea and asked, "What kind of games do you like to play?" They freely listed their favorites: Pictionary, Charades, Word Blender, and so forth. The group worker then suggested that the group members create a board game from scratch. They lit up at the idea and moved ahead. They created a game board and decided that each of the boxes on the board would represent a different feeling. They used an hourglass to keep time.

There were game cards in each category of the favorite games they had identified. For example, game cards for Charades might direct the player whose turn it was to act out a time when her or his dad was happy or sad or angry. Everything was about the person who died. The game pieces were handmade clay pieces that represented something memorable about their dads.

For example, one group member made a football ("Dad and I watched football on Sundays"). Another made an ice cream cone in remembrance of a special place they went to for ice cream "after my soccer games." And another made a sneaker because, "Dad jogged every morning." The group worker told the members that they could take the game pieces home each week but they declined because, as one of them said, "We want to keep them here because when we come here, that's when we play with our dads."

When dealing with trauma we are faced with two sides of the same coin: welcome remembrances and unwelcome reminders. Using activities in the group can help to elicit loving memories and can help to manage the stress of unwelcome reminders.

We need to do more than talk about trauma. We need to help our group members to identify symbols that enable them to grieve for what they've lost. The symbols don't have to be as grand and dramatic as, for example, the Yad Vashem Holocaust Memorial in Jerusalem or the Vietnam Veterans Memorial in Washington D.C. For group workers working with kids who have suffered traumatic losses, the symbols can be as elegantly simple as a handmade game piece for a board game – an ice cream cone, a sneaker, or football – to remember dad.

Creating space for all voices could mean using fewer words, and more symbols, action and activity. Like the groups of young people from settlement houses around New York City who organized to dump their old Nikes sneakers at shoe stores to protest the shoe company's double exploitation of the poor: paying workers in Indonesia only a few dollars a day and then charging urban teenagers exorbitant prices for their sneakers.

Creating space for all voices could mean using *less* curricula and *more* improvisation. Like the group of adolescent members of an LGBT coffeehouse and youth center who formed a creative arts group that created life-size high school lockers defaced with anti-gay slurs as a means of raising consciousness on a visceral level and promoting gay-straight alliances. The group members, using their expressive powers, took an important step towards advancing social justice.

Creating space for all voices could mean using *fewer* structured exercises and making space for *more* spontaneity and mutual aid. Like the group I had the privilege of meeting with, all of whom have roots in Haiti (Malekoff, 2014). I met with the group just weeks after the 2010 earthquake that toppled national landmarks and shantytown homes and killed and injured untold hundreds of thousands of people in and around the capital city Port-au-Prince. I asked them where they were when they heard about the disaster.

Sixteen-year-old Lynne said that when she got home, the phone rang. It was her father. He told her to get a glass of water. Then he asked her if she was sitting down. Next, he shared the heartbreaking news that her aunt Lynne was killed in the earthquake. The aunt she was named after, who was pregnant, had lost her life along with her unborn child when the earth opened up. The girl's eyes filled up and she said of her aunt – "We were like sisters."

Each one of the four girls and three boys learned about the earthquake when they arrived home after being together in an after-school program.

Eighteen-year-old Mahalia recalled, "When I got home my mom was crying. The TV was on. When I looked at the screen I saw a map of Haiti. There was a red dot."

I asked them about the media coverage and they said that it was both good and bad. "It was *good* to have updates," said 18-year-old Jean-Pierre, "but *bad* to see pictures of the dead and injured." The others nodded and Jean-Pierre said, "By the second day it felt like my family was going crazy" watching television. He said that the faces on the screen were hard to see clearly, leading them to wonder if anyone of them was a family member.

Jean-Pierre said that he tried to "move on" but discovered that it wasn't easy. "Each day when I go to school, I try to forget, but every day when I get there someone else is crying."

"How do you cope?" I asked. They turned to one another and gestured in a manner that emphasized their deep connection to one another. They talked about the support offered by groups of Haitian youths in school and in the community.

Osse, 16, said that it was important "to comfort one another and don't do anything reckless or lose control." I asked Osse what he meant by that. He said that some of their peers were insensitive and said hurtful things about Haiti.

Michel emphasized the importance of talking and not allowing one's feelings to get "all bunched up." I asked them if our get-together was helping to "un-bunch" their feelings a bit and they all nodded yes.

Long after we said goodbye, I had a distinct feeling of respect for this group of deeply empathic young people who had taken the first steps towards mutual aid and, by reaching out to support their peers, extended the bonds of belonging beyond the group.

In Conclusion

Group work is a tricky business and an important calling. Although we live in an era of evidence-based models, there are no foolproof solutions.

By all means get to know what works and what has been tested. Use the well-marketed models of practice and their manuals to guide you, but never to drive you.

Always tune in to the situational surround. Observe what it says about *that* moment in time that no curriculum can prepare you for. Trust your instincts. Take a chance. Work from the inside-out as well as the outside-in. Become co-creators with your group members. Take a risk and try something new. Be bold. Engage your group members as whole persons and not objects to be fixed. Lose your mind and come to your senses and get over yourself and go easy on yourself.

And, finally, I wish you a great weekend. Enjoy the presentations and workshops. Make the most of the space that you have in between the time you're listening to people like me. And remember that it's the intervals between the notes that can make all the difference. Thank you.

References

Alvarez, M. (2013, July 9). Meet the anti-cyber bullying teen squad: Harlem youth creating PSAs to tackle issue. *Newsday*, July 9, A32-A33.

King, M.L. (retrieved June 14, 2014). Daily Kos. Retrieved from http://www.dailykos.com/story/2012/04/04/1080503/-A-time-comes-when-silence-is-betrayal

Malekoff, A. (2014). *Group work with adolescents: Principles and practice* (3rd edition). New York: Guilford Press.

Malekoff, A. (2015, April). Bullies move from playground to cyberspace. *Long Island Weekly, Anton Community Newspapers.* Retrieved from http://www.longislandweekly.com/bullies-move-from-the-playground-to-cyberspace/

Miller, J. (2012). *Psychosocial capacity building in response to disaster,* New York: Columbia University Press.

Roman, C. (2002). It is not always easy to sit on your mouth. *Social Work with Groups*, 25:1/2, 61-64.

Stokowski, L. (n.d.) *Leopold Stokowski, Quotable quote.* Retrieved from https://www.goodreads.com/quotes/20488-a-painter-paints-pictures-on-canvas-but-musicians-paint-their

A Place in History: Adelphi NY Statewide Breast Cancer Hotline and Support Program

Erin Nau

Abstract: Breast cancer today is widely discussed in our communities and the options for support services are varied and pervasive. However, forty years ago breast cancer was not openly discussed among patients and their need for support was even more pressing than it is today. Founded in 1980, the Adelphi NY Statewide Breast Cancer Hotline and Support Program was the first program of its kind in New York State and one of the first in the country. This paper explores the history of the program, the theoretical perspectives that have guided the program, and the role of group work throughout the agency.

Introduction

Breast cancer today is widely discussed in our communities and the options for support services are varied and pervasive. However, forty years ago breast cancer was not openly discussed among patients and their need for support was even more pressing than it is today. Founded in 1980, the Adelphi NY Statewide Breast Cancer Hotline and Support Program was the first program of its kind in New York State and one of the first in the country.

Based on archival and personal testimony research, this paper explores the history of the program, the theoretical perspectives that have guided the program, and the role of group work throughout the agency. The study is based on archival materials, such as agency records and newsletters, and on interviews with the director of the program, social work staff members, and former group members who currently serve as volunteers.

Feminist Perspectives

Theoretical perspectives that have informed support groups for breast cancer survivors include relational feminist theory and empowerment theory. According to relational feminist theory, a "women's self-concept is based on mutual participation in a relationship; women's self-concept involves support given as well as support received" (Kayser, Sormanti, & Strainchamps, 1999, p. 272). A lack of support for women who are diagnosed with breast cancer may negatively impact their psychosocial well-being.

Despite changes to concepts of family and gender roles within families, women are often the caregivers in their families and social groups. In keeping with gender normative societal norms, women who believe that they must be self-sacrificing in a relationship may develop a "silence self-schema" that limits their ability to discuss their breast cancer with others (Kayser, Sormanti, & Strainchamps, 1999). They may try to shield their families from their fears or to take care of others before themselves. At the same time, however, women may feel disappointed when family and friends do not meet their expectations for support. Breast cancer support groups allow women to talk about these issues, challenging the silence self-schema by revealing the impact of silence on their lives.

In addition to the impact on their relationships, the diagnosis of breast cancer affects women's sense of self. Women describe how their worlds are completely changed after receiving the diagnosis of breast cancer by referring to a pre-diagnosis life and a post-diagnosis life. One of the goals of breast cancer support groups is to help women to feel empowered. Developing competence and confidence helps women advocate for themselves, even when they are feeling powerless (Stang & Mittlemark, 2010). Participants in support groups discuss their treatment options with one another and discover ways to advocate for the best available treatment. They also develop the confidence to ask questions about their treatment with their doctors.

Social workers facilitate breast cancer support groups from an empowerment perspective that seeks to strengthen participants at the intrapersonal, interactional, and behavioral levels (Zimmerman, 1995). Support group participants struggle with losing control and needing to do everything "right." They often find that sharing information is the most impactful part of joining a group. Learning with others encourages women to take control of their treatment, to advocate for themselves, and to become involved in community activities, such as educational events.

Responding to Need

According to breastcancer.org, one in eight women will be diagnosed with breast cancer in their lifetime (2015). Beginning in 1980, the rate of women who were diagnosed with breast cancer was higher than ever before, possibly as a result of the increased use of mammograms for detection (Zubko, 2012). The rising rate of breast cancer diagnoses did not immediately increase the opportunities for women to talk about their disease, however, and in 1980, women with a diagnosis of breast cancer had few options for support.

For residents of Long Island, New York, the rise in diagnosis in the 1980s was compounded by the higher incidence of breast cancer in Nassau and Suffolk Counties, which were identified as cancer cluster areas (Gammons et al., 2002; National Cancer Institute, 2013). A cancer cluster is defined as "the occurrence of a greater than expected number of cancer cases among a group of people in a defined geographic area over a specific time period" (National Cancer Institute, 2013). This higher rate of diagnosis led to an increase in needed psychosocial services related to a breast cancer in the region.

In response to the growing need, a group of social work faculty and interns at Adelphi University School of Social Work created a support group for women who were recovering from mastectomies. Support group participants felt isolated due to the stigma surrounding cancer, especially breast cancer, and they found comfort in discussing their fears, questions, and experiences with women who shared similar experiences. Research would later confirm that a positive exchange of support increases the psychological wellbeing of breast cancer survivors (Yoo et al., 2014).

The first breast cancer support groups were described as post-mastectomy groups, a name that suggests the taboo against speaking openly about breast cancer at that time. The goals of the groups were to help participants minimize emotional scaring and to speed up acceptance and adaptation. The post-mastectomy groups helped participants heal by giving and receiving support.

After having a positive experience supporting one another, members of the post-mastectomy groups helped initiate a hotline where women who were recently diagnosed could reach out to survivors for support. This was the beginning of the Adelphi NY Statewide Breast Cancer Hotline and Support Program, which today has the mission to educate, support, empower, and advocate for breast cancer patients, professionals, and the community (Adelphi, 2018). The hotline in conjunction with support groups allows women who are breast cancer survivors to help other women in similar situations.

The original post-mastectomy support groups were time-limited, close-ended groups that were facilitated by social workers. The small size of the groups, which consisted of no more than ten members, allowed for a sense of intimacy and safety. Social workers helped participants share information, normalize their experiences, and clarify medical advice given by other survivors. Group members raised such topics of discussion as relationships with families, particularly daughters and husbands; doctors, surgery and treatment; self-image; friendships; lovers and sexuality; and fears of recurrence.

Groups for Specific Populations

By the 1990s, the Adelphi breast cancer program began to branch out with support groups for specific populations. Support groups were offered for women younger than 35; women with a recurrence of breast cancer; women with Lymphedema; daughters of survivors; adolescent children of survivors; African American women with breast cancer; and women with metastatic breast cancer; men involved with breast cancer survivors; and men with breast cancer.

Some groups for specific populations addressed the needs of breast cancer survivors who were diagnosed at different ages or developmental phases of the life course. Younger women shared their fears about possibly not having children or living a full lifespan, while women in mid-life expressed concerns about the changes in their social and professional lives (Oktay & Walter, 1992; Thewes, Butow, Girgis, & Pendlebury, 2004).

The rate of breast cancer diagnosis in men is much lower than that of women, one in one thousand (American Cancer Society, 2016), and men describe a feeling of shock upon their diagnosis. Even men with a significant family history of breast cancer may feel immune from the disease. The support group for men with breast cancer allowed them to find support from their peers.

Groups for Women with Metastatic Breast Cancer: A Case Study

The needs of women with metastatic breast cancer, cancer which has also infected a secondary part of the body, are very different from those with a diagnosis of non-metastatic breast cancer. When Betty was diagnosed with breast cancer in her right breast, she had a mastectomy and was treated with chemotherapy and radiation. After taking oral hormone chemotherapy for five years, Betty was declared cancer free. Twelve years after her original diagnosis, however, a tumor was detected in Betty's kidney.

Betty had not participated in a support group after her original diagnosis, but she now was interested in finding support, and she joined a group of women who were recently diagnosed. Betty described the look on the other members' faces as horrified: "I was their worst fear." After the initial meeting, she reached out to the social worker to request a group for women with metastatic breast cancer. The social worker agreed, and the agency formed a support group for women with this specific need.

Although the first group session had only three members, participants felt relieved to speak with others who understood what they were going through. The metastatic breast cancer support group grew to ten active members, all sharing the ups and downs of their ongoing treatment and expressing similar feelings as their cancer worsened. Betty remained an active member of the metastatic breast cancer group for almost two years. She shared her experiences with clinical trials and her fear and sadness when her tumor grew because the current chemotherapy treatment had stopped working. Betty and other group members found that they could provide mutual aid to one another that no one else could offer. Although they valued support from family members and friends, they agreed that no one understands the experience as well as others the group.

An Evolving Program

As the Adelphi Breast Cancer Support Program moved into the new millennium, it evolved to meet survivors' changing needs. Today, an open-ended general support group for women with breast cancer allows women who are currently in treatment to meet with women who have been participating in the group for more than a year. Breast cancer survivors may experience emotional changes and anxiety about recurrence for many years after their initial diagnosis (Hodgkinson, 2007; Kayser, Sormanti, & Strainchamps, 1999), and the ongoing group allows women to return to the group whenever they feel the need for support.

Social workers who meet with survivors individually or in support groups identify their emerging issues and concerns, and the program responds by offering psychoeducational sessions for breast cancer survivors and their families and friends. Topics of community psychoeducational sessions have included ongoing emotional responses to a breast cancer diagnosis; body image and sexuality (Falk Dahl et al., 2010); and the value of seeking a second option regarding treatment (Bloom, Stewart, Chang, & Banks, 2004). In one recent session, a radiation oncologist responded to participant's questions and concerns about how to talk to their doctors. After the session, participants reported feeling more comfortable asking questions of their own doctors and even seeking second opinions.

The Role of Group Work

From its origin as a group for women who were recovering from a mastectomy, the Adelphi NY Statewide Breast Cancer Hotline and Support Program has relied on group work as its driving therapeutic intervention as well as the basis for organizational decision-making, professional development, and staff support. The small agency has no middle management, and the entire staff is included in task groups that make decisions related to agency policies and programs (Garvin & Galinsky, 2004). More than 100 volunteers, mostly breast cancer survivors, serve the program by answering the hotline and participating in community outreach and education. After completing a five-week orientation and training session, volunteers participate in monthly meetings, where they identify programmatic and community issues, and share strategies for helping newly diagnosed survivors.

Like volunteers, professional social workers alleviate the risk of burnout and compassion fatigue by giving and receiving mutual aid in groups (Keidel, 2002; Joinson, 1992). Group supervision allows social workers to share the burden of caring for persons who are very ill (Najjar, Davis, Beck-Coon, & Doebbeling, 2009). In addition to regularly scheduled group supervision, social workers offer spontaneous group supervision in response to particularly difficult situations.

A Place in History

The Adelphi NY Statewide Breast Cancer Hotline and Support Program has supported and empowered thousands of women through breast cancer support groups and other services. Participants have experienced first-hand what the research suggests – that groups provide significant support to women who are recovering from breast cancer (Stang & Mittlemark, 2002). The Adelphi program is staffed by experienced social workers and dedicated volunteers who are rooted in feminist perspectives and the method of social group work. In its nearly 40 year history, the agency has adapted to the changing needs of breast cancer survivors, and an annual survey is conducted to identify emerging community needs. Some principles remain constant, however. All support groups are free of charge to survivors, as they always have been. When survivors call the hotline, are referred by their oncologists, or learn about the program through community events, they are likely to find a group that responds to their specific needs. The Adelphi NY Statewide Breast Cancer Hotline and Support Program has secured a place in the history of supporting women diagnosed with breast cancer and will continue to serve them into the future.

References

Adelphi NY Statewide Breast Cancer Hotline and Support Program (2018). Retrieved from https://breast-cancer.adelphi.edu/

American Cancer Society. Breast Cancer Facts & Figures 2015-2016. Atlanta: American Cancer Society, Inc. 2015. Retrieved from https://www.cancer.org/research/cancer-facts-statistics/breast-cancer-facts-figures.html

Bloom, J. R., Stewart, S. L., Chang, S., & Banks, P. J. (2004). Then and now: Quality of life of young breast cancer survivors. *Psycho-Oncology, 13*(3), 147-160.

Gammon, M. D., Neugut, A. I., Santella, R. M., Teitelbaum, S. L., Britton, J. A., Terry, M. B., & Obrams, G. I. (2002). The Long Island Breast Cancer Study Project: Description of a multi-institutional collaboration to identify environmental risk factors for breast cancer. *Breast cancer research and treatment, 74*(3), 235-254.

Garvin, C. D., & Galinsky, M. J. (Eds.). (2004). *Handbook of social work with groups.* New York, NY: Guilford Press.

Holmberg, S. K., Scott, L. L., Alexy, W., & Fife, B. L. (2001). Relationship issues of women with breast cancer. *Cancer nursing, 24*(1), 53-60.

Joinson, C. (1992). Coping with compassion fatigue. *Nursing, 22*(4), 116-118.

Keidel, G. C. (2002). Burnout and compassion fatigue among hospice caregivers. *American Journal of Hospice and Palliative Medicine, 19*(3), 200-205.

National Cancer Institute (2013) Cancer Cluster Fact Sheet. Retrieved from https://www.cancer.gov/about-cancer/causes-prevention/risk/substances/cancer-clusters-fact-sheet#q1

Najjar, N., Davis, L. W., Beck-Coon, K., & Doebbeling, C. C. (2009). Compassion fatigue a review of the research to date and relevance to cancer-care providers. *Journal of Health Psychology, 14*(2), 267-277.

Oktay, J. S. & Water, C. A (1992). *Breast cancer in the life course: Women's experiences.* New York, NY: Springer.

Schover, L. R. (1991). The impact of breast cancer on sexuality, body image, and intimate relationships. *CA: A cancer journal for clinicians, 41*(2), 112-120.

Stang, I., & Mittelmark, M. B. (2010). Intervention to enhance empowerment in breast cancer self-help groups. *Nursing Inquiry, 17*(1), 47-57.

Taylor, S. E., Falke, R. L., Shoptaw, S. J., & Lichtman, R. R. (1986). Social support, support groups, and the cancer patient. *Journal of consulting and clinical psychology, 54*(5), 608.

Thewes, B., Butow, P., Girgis, A., & Pendlebury, S. (2004). The psychosocial needs of breast cancer survivors; a qualitative study of the shared and unique needs of younger versus older survivors. *Psycho-Oncology, 13*(3), 177-189.

Yoo, W., Namkoong, K., Choi, M., Shah, D. V., Tsang, S., Hong, Y., & Gustafson, D. H. (2014). Giving and receiving emotional support online: Communication competence as a moderator of psychosocial benefits for women with breast cancer. *Computers in human behavior, 30*, 13-22.

Zimmerman, M. A. (2000). Empowerment theory. In *Handbook of community psychology* (pp. 43-63). New York, NY: Springer.

Zimmerman M. A. (1995). Psychological empowerment: Issues and illustrations. *American Journal of Community Psychology 5*, 581–99.

Zubko, A. (2012). *Breast cancer occurrence, Diagnosis and mortality statistics.* Retrieved from https://www.maurerfoundation.org/breast-cancer-occurrence-diagnosis-mortality-statistics/

A Group Work Challenge to Maintain Group Purpose in an Open-Ended Group

Patricia Ki and Adina Muskat

This paper addresses a clinical group work challenge that occurred during an open-ended group for individuals pursuing or having completed bariatric (weight loss) surgery in a community-based hospital in the province of Ontario, Canada. The paper describes the bariatric surgery program; cites literature on maintaining group purpose in open-ended groups; and analyzes a clinical challenge that confronted the co-facilitators of the group. The paper seeks to inform future group work practice by considering the complex challenge of maintaining group purpose in open-ended groups.

The Bariatric Surgery Program

Bariatric (weight loss) surgery has been taking place for many years and in different forms throughout North America and the world. In 2009, the Ministry of Ontario (Toronto) Health and Long-Term Care (MOHLTC) began funding the surgery for residents of the province living with obesity and related medical conditions. The rationale behind this decision was an attempt to reduce costs expended on resources for patients in the health care system suffering from related symptoms, such as diabetes, high blood pressure, or cardiac issues. The ministry piloted the program to examine whether bariatric surgery would be a viable preventative measure in managing the long-term impact of obesity for individuals. One hospital in Toronto was selected as the central location for all assessment and follow-up support in the province of Ontario, although the surgeries were taking place at various hospitals throughout the province.

Because bariatric surgery is considered to be elective, individuals who choose to pursue it are required to have a referral from a health care provider and to undergo a thorough assessment process conducted by an interdisciplinary team of social workers, nurse practitioners, dieticians, psychologists, psychiatrists, and surgeons. This interdisciplinary team works collaboratively to explore a patient's readiness from a variety of perspectives including but not limited to life stressors; family and social support; mental health stability; finances; motivation for change; diet; and health history. As there are many diet and lifestyle changes required following bariatric surgery, it is also the responsibility of the team to educate and determine each patient's readiness to undergo the procedure in hopes of optimizing chances of long-term success. If the team finds that a patient is not ready for surgery, there are a variety of recommendations that must be followed in order for the patient to be considered again at a later point. Once an individual is determined ready for surgery and undergoes it, the team provides five years of holistic follow-up care to support patients with sustaining long-term changes.

While the majority of pre- and post-operative support takes place in individual meetings with an interdisciplinary team member, there are also a variety of groups that occur within the bariatric surgery program. Most of these groups are education-based and mandatory for patients to attend. While being considered for surgery, patients attend an orientation and nutrition group that addresses issues prior to surgery. Immediately after surgery, patients attend a one-month follow-up group facilitated by a dietician and a nurse which focuses on dietary and medical issues. In addition, post-surgical patients attend an 18-month follow-up group co-led by a psychologist and a social worker that examines ongoing motivation as well as social and emotional changes that commonly emerge after surgery.

The Open-Ended Support Group

In addition to the support groups already described, there is an open-ended support group that has been running since the inception of the Toronto Western Hospital Bariatric Surgery Program. The support group runs monthly in the evenings, and it is unique because it is open to all patients at any point in the pre- or post-surgery process. Group participation can number as many as 40 participants. The author is a member of the interdisciplinary team assigned by the hospital to take responsibility for facilitating this group one evening each month.

Participants in the open-ended support group are divided into two subgroups, a subgroup for longer-term participants who had bariatric surgery more than one year ago, and a subgroup for newer participants who have not yet had surgery or who had surgery within the past year. Various members of the interdisciplinary staff team assist with facilitating the two subgroups. Social workers and psychologists frequently take the lead in facilitating group sessions, while dieticians and nurses provide educational information and clarification of questions related to diet and medical issues.

Each group session begins in the same manner with participants of both subgroups meeting together briefly in a large private space in the hospital. A member of the interdisciplinary team welcomes members and explains the time schedule of the evening, general group rules, and other information. Following this brief larger meeting, the group divides into the two subgroups that meet for one hour. Each subgroup consists of approximately 20 participants. The subgroups come back together during the final 15 minutes of the evening, and a volunteer from each subgroup reports on the salient topics that were discussed. Each participant then completes a brief written evaluation of the experience.

The content of the subgroup sessions involves discussion topics generated by group participants. Facilitators help guide the conversation to elicit group members' shared experiences, give helpful information, and offer alternative perspectives. At times, facilitators may shift the conversation away from a particular topic in order to keep the group on track or to ensure that all topics of the evening are being addressed. Discussion topics are varied and wide-ranging, including such topics as emotional eating, body image, relationships, navigating work and social settings, medical complications, food intolerance, snack ideas, surgery disclosure, exercise, weight plateaus, and the unwanted return of detrimental eating habits.

A Challenge to Group Purpose

A group challenge occurred toward the end of a subgroup session for participants who had had their surgery more than one year ago. Some members of the subgroup proposed dividing into two smaller groups, one with those group members who had been successful in their weight-loss journey and one with those group members who were experiencing challenges. Participants who were challenged in their weight-loss journey suggested dividing the subgroup, because they found that hearing "success stories" of other group members was not helpful for them.

This suggestion posed a dilemma for the facilitators. Should the facilitators immediately agree to split the subgroup into two smaller groups, or should they confront the group to resolve the issue that had surfaced?

The group work literature explores the significance of group purpose in open-ended and closed-ended groups. Kurland and Salmon (2006) indicate that group purpose requires skillful use and understanding in order to be implemented effectively. Galinsky and Schopler (1985, 1989, 1994), who have written extensively on the subject of open-ended groups, explain that group purpose must be continuously negotiated and evaluated in open-ended groups. The ongoing nature open-ended groups requires that both group members and facilitators be consistently attuned to maintaining a defined purpose for the group.

With these considerations in mind, the co-facilitators met with the entire interdisciplinary team to discuss how best to resolve the group challenge related to group purpose in the open-ended support group. The interdisciplinary team suggested that the group should retain the original purpose of supporting group participants in both their successes and their struggles, but that the focus on this original purpose had been lost over time.

Based on the recommendations of the interdisciplinary team, the co-facilitators moved forward with meeting with the subgroup to try to resolve the issue that had been raised. The co-facilitators reminded participants of the original group purpose of providing mutual aid as group members sustain long-term lifestyle changes following bariatric surgery. The co-facilitators requested feedback from the group members on the possibility of remaining together as one group not only to share the "success stories" of some group members but also to provide validation for other group members who were having trouble identifying their own success stories during the recovery process. The group members agreed that sharing both successes and struggles was important to the goal of giving and receiving mutual support.

The group work challenge in the bariatric support group led to an evaluation and negotiation of group purpose. By naming the difficulties that they were experiencing in the subgroup session, participants reminded the group of its essential purpose and strengthened the mutual aid process. This will certainly not be the last time that a challenge to group purpose may arise in an open-ended group. We learn from the experience of the bariatric support group that such challenges help open-ended groups affirm their purpose and work together at a deeper level.

References

University Health Network (2016). About the Bariatric Clinic, Toronto Western Hospital. Retrieved from http://www.uhn.ca/Surgery/ PatientsFamilies/Clinics_Tests/Bariatric_Clinic

Galinsky, M. J., & Schopler, J. H. (1985). Patterns of entry and exit in open-ended groups. *Social Work with Groups, 8*(2), 67-80.

Galinsky, M. J., & Schopler, J. H. (1989). Developmental patterns in open-ended groups. *Social Work with Groups, 12*(2), 99-114.

Galinsky, M. J., & Schopler, J. H. (1994). Negative experiences in support groups. *Social Work in Health Care, 20*(1), 77-95.

Kurland, R., & Salmon, R. (1999). Purpose: A misunderstood and misused keystone of group work practice. *Social Work with Groups, 21*(3), 5-17.

Using Focus Groups to Inform Suicide Prevention Efforts on Campus

Willa J. Casstevens and Karen J. Miller

Suicide is a leading cause of death among college and university students in the USA. The suicide prevention program at North Carolina State University conducted student focus groups to help inform suicide prevention efforts at the university. Each of three focus groups was recruited from constituents deemed at higher risk for suicide than the general student population, including students who participate in Greek Life associations, students who identify with the LGBT community, and undergraduates. The focus groups asked NC State students about ways to increase student involvement with identifying suicide prevention strategies and developing and sustaining awareness-raising and prevention efforts on campus.

Introduction

Suicide prevention is particularly important in today's campus environment. In 2016, suicide "was the second leading cause of death among individuals between the ages of 10 and 34" in the USA (NIMH, 2018). Suicide is also the second leading cause of death among American college students (Eiser, 2011). The Garrett Lee Smith (GLS) Memorial Act, passed by Congress and signed into law in 2004, aimed to provide funding for suicide prevention programs to states, tribes, territories, and colleges and universities (Goldston, et al., 2010). A collaborative group at North Carolina State University initiated a campus suicide prevention program using internal seed money and obtained GLS funds to continue program development work. Program developers recognized the need for in-house, grassroots commitment, if long-term sustainability were to be achieved. This led the suicide prevention program to conduct a series of student focus groups. With approval from the university Institutional Review Board, the focus groups explored the question of how to increase student involvement in developing and sustaining suicide awareness-raising and prevention efforts on campus.

Method

Suicide prevention is an area where health and mental health overlap, and for many decades focus groups have been used to explore a variety of health-related topics (Redmond & Curtis, 2009). Focus groups have also been used to gain access to hard-to-reach constituencies with diverse populations and to discuss sensitive issues (e.g., Casstevens & Cohen, 2011; Jones et al., 2009; Napolitano, McCauley, Beltran, & Philips, 2002; Smith, Blake, Olson, & Tessaro, 2002; Tolliver, 2001). In the USA, the Centers for Disease Control and Prevention (CDC) collect data on suicide that has led to the identification of higher at-risk constituencies among youth. These constituencies include diverse populations, such as American Indians/Alaska Natives, and lesbian, gay, bisexual, and transgender (LGBT) youth (American Association of Suicidology, n.d.; Suicide Prevention Resource Center, 2008). Based on observations at NC State University, Greek Life (i.e., fraternity and sorority) members may be at greater risk than the general student body and undergraduates may be at greater risk than graduate students. Focus groups presented a way to explore views and perceptions within some of these different constituencies.

Three focus groups were formed, and each focus group was recruited from students who identified with a particular higher-risk constituency: 1) Greek Life associations, 2) the LGBT community, and 3) undergraduates. Recruitment occurred through flyers, departmental listserv emails, sign-up sheets at related events or locations, and word-of-mouth. It was expected that some participants might identify with more than one constituency, for example an undergraduate student might also identify as a member of a Greek Life association and or the LGBT community. Follow-up with potential participants was accomplished either by email or phone to assure that participants were at least 18 years of age and that they identified as members of the targeted constituency for the group they attended.

Three groups were scheduled during spring semester 2014, providing one 90-minute session with each constituency. During focus groups, leaders asked participants the following questions regarding suicide prevention approaches at the university:

1. Are you aware of any suicide awareness-raising or prevention efforts?
2. What would help raise awareness about suicide and its prevention?
3. What can students do to help with awareness and prevention efforts?
4. What can students or student groups do to become a pivotal or key part of suicide awareness and prevention efforts?
5. Do you have any other ideas or thoughts on this you'd like to share?

These questions were followed as needed by pre-determined prompts (Appendix 1). At the end of the groups, each participant was given a donated T-shirt to thank them for their time. Focus groups were audio-recorded and the recordings transcribed. A note-taker was present during each group, and a laptop was used for note-taking. Research assistants independently reviewed and coded each transcript. Coding focused on what students can do to help with suicide awareness and prevention efforts and to become key parts of those efforts at the university. Results were used to enhance program development and promote student involvement in suicide prevention efforts.

Results

Focus group participants identified strategies for awareness-raising, as well as areas for student involvement. Strategies for awareness-raising were presented at the NC State 2014 Summer Undergraduate Research Symposium (Premo, 2014). Areas related to student involvement were presented at the 10th Annual State of North Carolina Undergraduate Research and Creativity Symposium (Eudy, 2014).

The focus groups discussed individual, organizational, and collaborative strategies for increasing student involvement. Individually, students can volunteer at suicide prevention and related outreach events, such as the annual candlelight vigil on World Suicide Prevention Day, and they can take *QPR Gatekeeper Training for Suicide Prevention*, an evidence-based program that is offered at no cost to students, staff, faculty, and administrators by certified trainers on campus. Students can sponsor a survivor of suicide loss support group or work to make the campus counseling center waiting room warmer and more inviting, for example, by creating posters with inspirational quotes. Students also can help educate parents and reach out to families through letters and community work. They can create a community event, such as a symposium, pep rally, or commemoration, and distribute educational brochures and flyers.

In order to help reduce the stigma associated with help-seeking and mental health concerns, students can work towards becoming aware of their surroundings and the people around them, and they can offer support or challenge avoidance behaviors. Students can sponsor a "watch our words" movement, educate peers one-on-one, speak out against stigma, and hold peers accountable for negative comments. Students may be willing to share personal experiences at presentations and outreach events. They can promote awareness and education through advertising, word of mouth, and newsletters, and they can create videos or skits about college stress and depression to help educate students. Developing a buddy or peer mentoring program, and finding on-campus advocates were also mentioned. Student organizations need to advertise and keep the messaging "in people's faces" as well as partner on collaborative events across campus. Various local and campus events were mentioned as fruitful grounds for collaboration.

Discussion

Focus group participants brought combatting stigma related to mental health difficulties to the table, as well as suicide prevention. This may be a testament to the university counseling center's concurrent and widespread "Stop the Stigma" campaign. Focus group project limitations involved recruitment, which led to small group sizes. The group of undergraduates had six participants, and the group of Greek Life members and LGBT community members had three participants each. Due to time and funding constraints, it was decided to proceed with the small groups of Greek Life and LGBT participants. The groups were exploratory in nature and not intended to be representative of the populations involved. It was hoped that data obtained could contribute to program development, and indeed this occurred.

Consultation after the data analysis led those involved in the focus group project to make the following recommendations to the campus suicide prevention program:

- Increase the number of events participated in or sponsored
- Involve more student organizations in outreach efforts
- Hold more suicide prevention trainings
- Advertise university counseling center resources more widely
- Continue to train and support residence hall advisors and staff
- Advocate for requiring suicide awareness training in courses and curricula.

Subsequent consultation among concerned students led to the development of a brief talk that students could share in classes with instructor permission. The talk was written in 2014 by graduating senior Sara Hamilton. This idea became a whole new project, the *2-Minute Talk Program* which was approved by the counseling center, sponsored by a student organization, and successfully piloted (Casstevens, Aggarwal, Eudy, & Risher, 2015). In spite of limitations, the focus group series offered both recommendations and a valuable programmatic addition to suicide prevention at the university.

Acknowledgements

The authors extend thanks to and acknowledge the assistance of: H. Dawes, M. Eudy, S. Hamilton, & K. N. Premo. Funding for the focus groups came from a North Carolina State University College of Humanities and Social Sciences' Undergraduate Research Grant in 2013-14. The NC State University suicide prevention program would not have been possible without a North Carolina State University Office of Extension, Engagement and Economic Development Seed Grant in 2011-12, and subsequent Grant Number 1U79SM060507-10 from the Substance Abuse and Mental Health Services Administration (SAMHSA), U.S. Department of Health and Human Services (HHS); Dr. J. K. Hall is the Co-Investigator on these grants. The views, policies, and opinions expressed are those of the authors and do not necessarily reflect those of SAMHSA, HHS, or NC State University.

References

American Association of Suicidology (n.d.). Youth suicidal behavior fact sheet 4.11final.docx. Retrieved from: www.sprc.org/sites/sprc.org/files/library/YouthSuicidalBehavior.pdf

Casstevens, W. J., Aggarwal, A., Eudy, M., Risher, A. C. (October, 2015). *The "2Minute Talk" student volunteer program launched by NAMI on Campus at NC State.* Workshop presented at NAMI-NC Annual Conference: Transforming the Face of Mental Illness in North Carolina, Raleigh, North Carolina.

Casstevens, W. J., & Cohen, M. B. (2011). A group work approach to focus group research in the context of a psychiatric clubhouse program. *Groupwork 21*(1), 46- 58.

Centers for Disease Control and Prevention (2013). *Ten leading causes of death by age group, United States – 2013.* Retrieved from: www.cdc.gov/injury/wisqars/pdf/leading_causes_of_death_by_age_group_2013-a.pdf

Eiser, A. (September, 2011). The crisis on campus: APA is working with Congress to address serious mental health problems on college campuses. *Monitor on Psychology, 42*(8), 18.

Eudy, M. (2014, Nov. 22). Students Can Raise Awareness and Help Prevent Suicide. Poster session at the 10th Annual State of North Carolina Undergraduate Research and Creativity Symposium, North Carolina State University, Raleigh, North Carolina. Faculty Advisor: W. J. Casstevens.

Goldston, D. B., Walrath, C. M., McKeon, R., Puddy, R. W., Lubell, K. M., Potter, L. B., & Rodi, M. S. (2010). The Garrett Lee Smith Memorial suicide prevention program. *Suicide Life Threatening Behavior, 40*(3), 245-256.

Jones, A. R., Hyland, R. M., Parkinson, K. N., Adamson, A. J., & The Gateshead Millennium Study Core Team (2009). Developing a focus group approach for exploring parents' perspectives on childhood overweight. *Nutrition Bulletin, 34,* 214-219.

Napolitano, M., McCauley, L., Beltran, M. & Philips, J. (2002). The dynamic process of focus groups with migrant farm workers: The Oregon experience. *Journal of Immigrant Health, 4*(4), 177-182.

National Institute of Mental Health (May, 2018). *Health information statistics: Suicide.* Retrieved from: www.nimh.nih.gov/health/statistics/suicide. shtml

Premo, K. (2014, April 14). Suicide Prevention Focus Groups with Students. Poster session at the NC State 2014 Summer Undergraduate Research Symposium, North Carolina State University, Raleigh, North Carolina. Faculty Advisors: J. K. Hall & W. J. Casstevens.

Redmond, R. & Curtis, E. (2009). Focus groups: Principles and process. *Nurse Researcher, 16*(3), 57-69.

Smith, S. L., Blake, K., Olson, C. R., & Tessaro, I. (2002). Community entry in conducting rural focus groups: Process, legitimacy, and lessons learned. *The Journal of Rural Health, 18*(1), 118-123.

Suicide Prevention Resource Center (2008). *Suicide risk and prevention for lesbian, gay, bisexual, and transgender youth.* Newton, MA: Education Development Center, Inc. Retrieved from: www.sprc.org/sites/sprc.org/ files/library/SPRC_LGBT_Youth.pdf

Tolliver, D. E. (2001). African American female caregivers of family members living with HIV/AIDS. *Families in Society: The Journal of Contemporary Human Services, 82*(2), 145-156.

Appendix
Focus Group Script and Instructions

Focus Group Stage	Facilitator Script	Accompanying Instructions
Opening the focus group:	*Hi and welcome everyone! We really appreciate your taking time to be with us today.* *My name is _____ and I'll be facilitating our focus group today. We also have _____ with us – she will be taking notes during the discussion.* *Can we take a minute to introduce ourselves? Your names won't be taken down in the notes – we just want to get acquainted before we start.*	Give people time to go round the table and introduce themselves – no audio-recording devices should be turned on yet.
	Great, thanks! *Your input on campus suicide prevention is really important to us and we will be audio-recording the focus group to make sure we don't miss anything.* *Since this is being audio-recorded and may be used in faculty research, we need give you an information sheet for informed consent purposes. You don't need to sign it, but please take a minute to review it. I'll do my best to answer any questions.*	Let people take a minute to read and ask/answer questions – at this point if anyone objects to the audio-recording and their concerns cannot be sufficiently addressed, you can turn off recording devices and simply agree to go with note-taking.

Facilitating group discussion:	*Okay, let's get started. I'm here to facilitate the group, and have several questions to help focus our discussion. Our goal is to get your ideas on how students can get involved, or more involved, with the NC State suicide prevention program, because suicide's now the second leading cause of death among college students in the US.* *To start off,*	
	Are you aware of any suicide awareness-raising or prevention efforts at NC State University? Prompt, to use only if necessary: *If so, please share them with the group!*	Let the discussion flow – do NOT interject remarks. Especially do not interject comments like "yes, we're doing that" "we tried that and it didn't work, so we stopped" etc.
	Reminder, to use only if necessary: *I'm just here as group facilitator – we can talk about that after the group if you want!*	If participants ask you direct questions, you can remind them of your role by using this statement.
	Great discussion, thanks!	After the discussion trails off/slows down, make this comment.
	What would help raise awareness about suicide and its prevention at NC State University?	Let the discussion flow – do NOT interject remarks. Especially do not interject comments like "yes, we're doing that already" "we tried that and it didn't work" "that won't work because…"

	Only if true, comment: *Love the ideas – thanks!*	After the discussion trails off/slows down, and only if it is true, you can make this comment.
	What can students do to help with awareness and prevention efforts at NC State? Prompt, to use only if necessary: *What are the next steps to make this happen?*	
	What can students or student groups do to become a pivotal or key part of suicide awareness and prevention efforts at NC State? Prompt, to use only if necessary: *What are the next steps to make this happen?*	This question may not be necessary, but if the discussion slows, ask it.
Closing the group:	*Thanks for all the ideas everyone! As we wrap up,*	As discussion slows, about 10 minutes before the end of the group.
	Do you have any other ideas or thoughts on this you'd like to share?	
	We have some resource brochures on suicide prevention and alcohol use that we'd like to share with you.	Pass out brochures.
	Also, we'd like to say "thank you" by giving you a T-shirt – so please stay afterwards and pick out your size!	

Professional Development: An MSW Course Based on Group Work Principles and Opportunities

Shirley R. Simon

Abtract: Professional development is a critical but frequently overlooked aspect of students' education. This paper chronicles a group work-based MSW elective course that explores issues of professional identity and responsibility within a contemporary context, develops projects focused on individually-determined professional interests, and provides opportunities to participate in and present at professional conferences such as the International Association for Social Work with Groups (IASWG) Symposium. The syllabus, feedback from students, and recommendations for replication are shared.

Introduction

Social work is a unique and complicated profession. Graduates of our programs face myriad societal misconceptions and faulty expectations. Moreover, emerging professionals today experience greater workloads with less supervision and onsite continuing education than in previous decades (Whitaker, Weismiller & Clark, 2006; Bergart & Simon, 2004). Yet, opportunities for professional contribution, connection, and advancement abound. The question is, "Are we adequately preparing our students with the knowledge, skills, and resources to optimize their professional development and meet professional challenges?"

The author, a faculty member at a large Midwestern social work program, grappled with this question. A review of the literature revealed a long-standing struggle with this issue in other professional fields (Cruess & Cruess, 1997; Eitzen, 1988; Heflinger & Doykos, 2016; Ledet, Esparza, & Peloquin, 2005; Ducheny et al., 1997). Even the definition of professional development has been the subject of debate and question (Buysse, Winton, & Rous, 2009; Ducheny et al., 1997). Articles that address professional development frequently neglect to define the concept but concur that there is no one model or framework for understanding and promoting this topic (Heflinger & Doykos, 2016; Ledet, Esparza, & Peloquin, 2005).

A review of the social work literature finds little discussion of professional development. Neither the *Social Work Dictionary, 6th ed.* (Barker, 2014) nor *the Encyclopedia of Social Work, 20th ed.* (Mizrahi & Davis, 2008) contains a definition of professional development. What is written relates to continuing professional education or efforts that take place post-graduation. The Council on Social Work Education's Educational Policy and Accreditation Standards (EPAS, 2015) clearly address the concept that the curriculum should shape professional character and competence, but only mention professional development within the context of "implicit curriculum," referring to the beneficial effects of students participating in academic and student affairs policy-making (p.14) and the manner in which faculty demonstrate their ongoing professional development (p. 16). While a definition of professional development within the field of social work is not readily accessible and thus warrants further critical exploration, Ducheny et al. (1997) offer a definition for the field of psychology that could pertain to social work. They define professional development as "an ongoing process through which an individual derives a cohesive sense of professional identity by integrating the broad-based knowledge, skills, and attitudes within psychology [social work] with one's values and interests" (p. 89).

If students are to value and operationalize their ongoing effective professional development, shouldn't this be a deliberate component of MSW education? Since the MSW is historically the terminal degree within social work, MSW graduates should be prepared with the values, resources, and skills to embark upon and maintain their professional development. The dearth of social work literature on the professional development of social work students, the licensing and career expectations of our graduates, and the very needs of our profession and professional associations affirm the need to address this issue.

Background

The author's prior efforts to link students and professional associations, to provide opportunities for students' peer reviewed presentations, and to motivate students' ongoing professional development (Simon, Webster, & Horn, 2007) led to the conclusion that both curricular and extracurricular opportunities to focus on issues of professional development are important. Given the busy and complex time commitments and obligations of the typical MSW student, extracurricular opportunities, no matter how compelling, are often ignored. The author determined that it was important to approach this issue from a curricular vantage point and began by developing a curricular module embedded in a required MSW group work course that addressed one component of this concept – professional associations and their potential opportunities for professional development. Both quantitative and qualitative assessments of this module indicated that students experienced increased knowledge of and appreciation for the role of professional associations. The module facilitated enthusiasm for the profession, provided opportunities to join professional associations, and inspired self-confidence and motivation to assume professional leadership positions (Simon, 2012; Simon & Grossman, in press).

It became clear, however, that this was only one aspect of students' well-rounded grasp of and commitment to lifelong professional development. More focused attention needed to be directed to a deeper and more holistic engagement with the concept. With the encouragement of students who had attended and presented at association conferences, the author utilized her group work expertise to design and implement a cohort model elective MSW course entitled "Professional Development." The course began as a special topics elective, evolved to be a yearly elective option, and is now a core component of a sub-specialization in group work. This paper chronicles the development of, rationale for, and group work principles that provide the framework for an MSW course on Professional Development.

Course Description

This Professional Development course focuses on the student's unique development as a social work professional. It encourages reflection, assessment, and skill building aimed at creating a foundation for lifelong professional growth. The course combines elements of group cohesion, mutual aid, and task group principles to create an environment and setting that stimulates personal and professional exploration. It requires participation in a professional association conference, such as the IASWG Symposium, and incorporates a semester-long individually designed project that aims to facilitate students' next steps in their professional journeys. Course units include: the profession of social work – identity, opportunities and responsibilities; professional associations; group work, teamwork, and collaboration in professional practice; making a professional presentation; preparing and submitting a manuscript for publication; ongoing professional development; and developing a personal plan for professional development.

A primary goal of this Professional Development course is to empower students and support their shift in thinking from a passive consumer of instructor-provided information and direction to a more independent, self-motivated professional perspective. The first few course sessions are instructor led, but increasingly large components of course sessions are facilitated by students. Each of the following assignments is structured to facilitate the objectives of the course and encourage engagement and cooperative learning.

Course Assignments

Professional Development Project

For this assignment, students are asked to reflect upon their professional and educational experiences and identify areas for further development. With collaboration and support from instructor and classmates, students determine and focus on one area of professional interest for the duration of the course. They identify learning objectives, develop concrete methods to achieve these objectives, and design and complete a project demonstrating outcomes. Projects range from traditional research papers, to preparing and presenting a poster at a conference, to interviewing or shadowing social workers in an area of career interest.

Attendance at a 2-3 day Social Work/Social Welfare Professional Conference

This assignment requires students to learn about, participate in, and reflect upon a professional association gathering related to their career interests. Conferences selected include those sponsored by the International Association of Social Work with Groups (IASWG), National Association of Social Workers (NASW), American Group Psychotherapy Society (AGPS), Council on Social Work Education (CSWE), School Social Workers of America (ASA), American Society on Aging (ASA), International Federation of Social Workers (IFSW), and more.

Student Partnerships

Each student is paired with a classmate of her or his choosing. These pairings have three objectives: to facilitate the completion of each partner's professional development project, to support the partner's preparation for and facilitation of a class discussion on assigned readings, and to support and enhance the partner's conference/symposium experience.

Presentations

Students are assigned to deliver presentations individually and in pairs:

• Student pairs lead the class in a discussion of assigned readings.

Each pair prepares discussion questions and a feedback form.
- Each student delivers a brief presentation to a component of the University community (a class, orientation program, alumni group etc.) about their professional expertise, the experience of participating in a professional conference/symposium, or their professional development project.
- Each student prepares a 30 second "elevator speech" describing the profession of social work. Students present their speech to the class and to one other non-social work individual.

Journals

Each student submits two journals – a reading journal and a course and conference journal:

- In the reading journal, students identify and explain their learning "take aways" and questions raised by the required course readings.
- In the course and conference journal, students reflect upon their experiences within the course and at the conference and relate these experiences to course readings and discussions.

Group Work Considerations and Inclusions

The Professional Development course, facilitated seminar style, is built largely upon the following group work considerations: contracting; empowerment; safe, inclusive environment; clarity of purpose; cohesion; mutual aid; and the therapeutic/helping factors of groups.

The class itself is viewed as a group in which engagement and participation are primary. Attention is focused on creating a safe, non-hierarchical environment where diversity of opinion and experience are welcome. To facilitate engagement and enhance participation, the rationale and purpose for each of the assignments is shared. The course is predicated upon the premise that the students are adult learners entitled to understand the rationale behind each of the course expectations. Although the course structure and assignments are largely predetermined, each cohort is unique, and the course builds in flexibility near the end of the term to address the shared interests of the particular cohort. Suggestions for the focus of these sessions – topics, speakers, field experiences – are solicited from the class, thereby highlighting the importance and desirability of student input and engagement.

During the first class sessions, a class contract is established based upon the syllabus and a discussion of verbal expectations. Inclusion and respect for one another are emphasized. Within the contracting process, the instructor clarifies the purpose of the course as a vehicle for empowering students to take charge of their own learning. Student partnerships also create written contracts to define and outline mutual expectations and communication methods. Both the class and partnership contracts are revisited and assessed toward the end of the course.

In order to begin to build community within the class, a welcome letter sharing the philosophy and structure of the course is emailed to each student prior to the first class. Within this letter, two of the major assignments – conference attendance and professional development project – are described and students are asked to bring their initial thoughts to class. A list of professional associations and their upcoming conferences is attached to this letter. During the first class, as an icebreaker, students verbally introduce themselves, identifying anticipated professional development project topics and potential conference attendance. Receiving feedback and suggestions from peers on the first day of class affirms the interdependent focus of the class. Periodically during the semester there are check-ins regarding these assignments, and students have an opportunity to hear what their peers are doing and simultaneously receive feedback. Also, an initial assignment asks students to develop and post a three to four slide PowerPoint presentation introducing themselves and their backgrounds, interests, and professional goals. Students are then asked to respond to one another's posts via online messages. When students later form semester-long partnerships, they are requested to review the presentations of their partners. Each of these assignments and subsequent interactions contribute to the development of a group cohort and a spirit of mutual aid.

Assignments and discussions are also aimed at building cohesion, empowerment, and mutual aid. While the first few sessions are instructor led, the later course sessions are increasingly facilitated by students. Structurally this is done by having self-selected pairs of students lead class discussions about the required readings. Initially, the instructor models the facilitation process, and students are then requested to follow the model. The facilitation focuses on group engagement and discussion of relevant material rather than a lecture about the reading content. Because students are required to complete a reading journal identifying takeaways from the assigned articles prior to the class presentations, they have a working knowledge of the topics being discussed. In addition, the majority of required readings are selected because of their relevance to students' own professional development. Hence, students can be expected to be active, informed participants.

Yalom's therapeutic factors of groups (2015) are imbedded in the class and the interactions with the instructor. Universalization, instillation of hope, imparting information, cohesion, altruism, interpersonal learning, and even a bit of catharsis can be found within course interactions. Students feel a sense of being "in the same boat," as they share their academic and professional questions and concerns and their attempts to plan and to address professional aspirations. They glean hope from one another, from the sense that others are navigating similar career paths and from the specific information, opportunities, and direction provided throughout the course. Imparting information takes place didactically through readings, presentations, and individual projects, as well as interpersonally via student-to-student and student-to-instructor interactions. Cohesion is typically seen as the course develops and students seek each other out both within and outside of the classroom. The language within the class often quickly transitions from "the course" and "you," to "we" and "us." Altruism evolves as participants share resources and referrals and give feedback to one another within the partnerships and in the group as a whole. Students also find it helpful to be able to vent to their peers about their struggles and frustrations within the field while simultaneously receiving support for their efforts and suggestions about next steps.

Outcomes

Although long-term studies on the effectiveness of this Professional Development class have not been conducted, the initial assessments based on course evaluations, anecdotal comments, and instructor feedback appear to support its value. The student course evaluations, spanning multiple years, consistently rank the class "outstanding." Students comment on the course's personal and professional relevance, the value of the professional association connection, and the cohesive seminar learning environment. Examples of these qualitative comments include:

This course was one of the best courses that I had in the MSW program, in that the focus was on how I was developing professionally. It was relevant to my life and career now.

The learning style of this course was very different from other courses. It made learning specific to meet my strengths and weaknesses. It challenged and enhanced the way I see myself as a professional.

I appreciated the professor's respect for us as self-directed and capable professionals. It gave me a lot of confidence moving into my professional worth.

The assignment to connect with a professional association and attend a conference was the richest learning experience of my coursework so far.

I appreciated the opportunity to direct personal learning in a way that addressed my passions and interests. The seminar format made for an enjoyable experience in which I felt heard and valuable to discussion. The professor was passionate about the topic and her enthusiasm was contagious. Overall, I thought the course provided an enriching experience which furthered my professional skills, knowledge, and confidence.

From the instructor's perspective, the course also appears to be effective. The students seem consistently engaged with the material and with one another, and they readily make suggestions about course activities. Their comfort with the elements of becoming a professional heightens as the course unfolds. With rare exception, the students report that the professional association conference is one of the highlights of their master's program. It is truly a pleasure to teach this course and watch as students' self-confidence and professional development evolve.

Considerations for Replication

It is hoped that this course can be replicated or incorporated within other curricular components of social work programs. Some considerations for doing so effectively include:

- Determining whether there is an instructor comfortable with and committed to this group work based, seminar-style of teaching.
- Assessing whether this topic and approach should stand alone as a separate elective course or are best incorporated into fieldwork seminars or capstone courses.
- Reviewing the wide range of topics that pertain to the broad concept of professional development.
- Investigating funding supports for student participation in professional conferences. While students may be able to minimize costs by volunteering at conferences and/or by finding local conferences to attend, the provision of stipends or other financial supports could be helpful.

Conclusion

Professional development is certainly a topic meriting further attention within social work education. Laying a foundational basis for lifelong involvement and commitment to one's professional growth and contributions is a laudable goal. Whether enrolling in a Professional Development course contributes to this goal is yet to be determined via long-term studies; nevertheless, course evaluations, self-reports and anecdotal observations attest to its value for numerous cohorts of students. As detailed within this paper, the course provides a group work-based vehicle for integrating a professional development focus within social work curricula and calls attention to this overlooked aspect of MSW students' education.

Acknowledgement

The author would like to thank Stephanie Drozd, MSW, for her support and assistance in preparing this manuscript.

References

Barker, R. (2014). *The social work dictionary* (Sixth Ed.). Washington, DC: NASW Press.

Bergart, A. M. and Simon, S. R. (2004). Practicing what we preach: Creating groups for ourselves. *Social Work with Groups, 27(4),* 17-30.

Buysse, V., Winton, P., & Rous, B. (2009). Reaching consensus on a definition of professional development for the early childhood field. *Topics in Early Childhood Special Education, 28*(4), 235-243. Retrieved from https://loyola-primo.hosted.exlibrisgroup.com/primo-explore/ fulldisplay?docid=TN_sagej10.1177_0271121408328173&context=P C&vid=01LUC&search_scope=Library_Collections&tab=default_ tab&lang=en_US

Council on Social Work Education. (2015). Educational Policy and Accreditation Standards for Baccalaureate and Master's Social Work Programs. Retrieved from https://www.cswe.org/getattachment/ Accreditation/Accreditation-Process/2015-EPAS/2015EPAS_Web_ FINAL.pdf.aspx

Cruess, S. R. and Cruess, R. L. (1997). Professionalism must be taught. *British Medical Journal, 315,* 1674-1677.

Ducheny, K., Alletzhauser, H. L., Crandell, D., & Schneider, T. R. (1997). Graduate student professional development. *Professional Psychology: Research And Practice, 28*(1), 87-91. Retrieved from http://flagship.luc.edu/login?url=http://search.ebscohost.com/login. aspx?direct=true&db=pdh&AN=1997-02162-015&site=ehost-live

Eitzen, D. S. (1988). The introduction of graduate students to the profession of sociology. *Teaching Sociology, 16,* 279-283.

Heflinger, C., & Doykos, B. (2016). Paving the pathway: Exploring student perceptions of professional development preparation in doctoral education. *Innovative Higher Education, 41*(4), 343-358. Retrieved from http://flagship.luc.edu/login?url=http://search.ebscohost.com/login.asp

x?direct=true&db=ehh&AN=116859690&site=ehost-live

Ledet, L., Esparza, C., & Peloquin, S. (2005). The conceptualization, formative evaluation, and design of a process for student professional development. *The American Journal of Occupational Therapy, 59*(4), 457-66. Retrieved from https://loyola-primo.hosted.exlibrisgroup.com/primo-explore/ fulldisplay?docid=TN_medline16124212&context=PC&vid=01LUC&s earch_scope=Library_Collections&tab=default_tab&lang=en_US

Mizrahi, T., & Davis, L. (2008). *Encyclopedia of social work* (20th ed.). Washington, D.C.: NASW Press.

Simon, S. R. (2012). Connecting students and professional associations: A curricular approach. In G.T. Tully, K. Sweeney, & S. Palombo (Eds.), Groups: Gateways to growth: Proceedings of the 29th International Symposium on Social Work with Groups (pp. 139-159). London: Whiting and Birch Ltd.

Simon, S.R. & Grossman, S. (in press). Linking students and professional associations: A curricular strategy. *Journal of Practice Teaching & Learning.*

Simon, S. R., Webster, J., & Horn, K. (2007). A critical call for connecting students and professional organizations. *Social Work with Groups: A Journal of Community and Clinical Practice, 30*(4), 5-19.

Whitaker,T,Weismiller,T., & Clark, E. (2006). Assuring the sufficiency of a frontline workforce: A national study of licensed social workers: Executive summary. Washington, DC: National Association of Social Workers. Retrieved from https://www.socialworkers.org/LinkClick.asp x?fileticket=QKU6bvt6Rwc%3D&portalid=0

Yalom, I., & Leszcz, M. (2005). *The theory and practice of group psychotherapy* (5th ed.). New York: Basic Books.

Remembering Jim Garland: Loneliness in the Group

Lorrie Greenhouse Gardella

James A. Garland, Sr. (1929-2012) integrated the sociological and political perspectives of social group work with the psychodynamic perspectives of clinical practice. During his 40-year career at Boston University School of Social Work, he mentored generations of students and faculty while also maintaining a group work practice, holding professional leadership positions, and consulting with health and human services organizations throughout the greater Boston area. Drawing on oral history interviews, this paper reviews Garland's published and unpublished perspectives on group work and group development in the context of his professional identity formation as a social worker.

Social work educator James A. Garland (1929-2012), who entered social work during the settlement house era, integrated the sociological and political perspectives of social group work with the psychodynamic perspectives of clinical practice. In a career spanning more than 40 years, he mentored generations of students and faculty at Boston University School of Social Work while maintaining a group work practice, holding professional leadership positions, and consulting with health and human services organizations throughout the greater Boston area. Co-author of the influential "Model for Stages of Development in Social Work Groups" (Garland, Jones & Kolodny, 1965), later known as the Boston model, Jim Garland considered his most significant publication to be "Loneliness in the Group: An Element of Treatment" (1986), which explored the experience of loss as a therapeutic resource. In his later career, Jim preferred "the intimacy of direct teaching and consulting" to academic writing, and his emerging insights on group work in organizations were left to the unrecorded memories of his colleagues, students, and clients. Based on the methodology of oral history research (Martin, 1995; Kayser & Morrissey, 1998), this paper reviews Garland's published and unpublished perspectives on social group work in the context of his professional identity formation as a social worker.

I conducted oral history interviews with Jim Garland on August

18 and September 15, 1998, just after he had retired from Boston University. As defined by the Oral History Association (2018):

> Oral history interviews seek an in-depth account of personal experience and reflections, with sufficient time allowed for the narrators to give their story the fullness they desire. The content of oral history interviews is grounded in reflections on the past . . .

I first met with Jim in his Boston University office as he was packing up his personal papers and belongings. Each new stack of papers sparked memories of his career. When we continued the interview a few weeks later, I spent the day with Jim in his home in Mansfield, Massachusetts, where he made me his "world-famous" marinara sauce with raisins. I rode home on the train carrying notes, audio-tapes, and a large jar of sauce.

The transcripts of our conversations served as the basis for an oral history that presented Jim's reflections in his own words, though edited for clarity and organization. Jim was gratified by the resulting oral history – "Now, I have the story of my life!" I wondered, however, about the longer term significance of his work. How will Jim Garland's contributions be remembered and applied by future generations? By exploring his published research in light of his unpublished reflections, this paper offers a developmental perspective on Jim Garland's professional identity formation. In addition, it raises questions about the role and responsibility of IASWG in preserving the published and unpublished practice wisdom of group workers.

Pre-affiliation Stage: "A Model for Stages of Development in Social Work Groups"

The 1965 publication of "A Model for Stages of Development in Social Work Groups," by Jim Garland and his colleagues Hubert (Hubie) Jones and Ralph Kolodny, represented a milestone in the history of social work research (Northern, 2004) and "a seminal, pioneering contribution to the theory and practice of social group work" (Bartolomeo, 2009). The authors, who later served together at Boston University School of Social Work, based their developmental model on a systematic study of long-term children's groups that were conducted by the Department of Neighborhood Clubs of the Boston Children's Service Association from 1959 through 1963.

Hubie Jones, who would later serve as dean of Boston University School of Social Work, remembered Jim's role as lead author of the study (personal communication, September 25, 2015):

> *Jim was a brilliant clinician and theoretical thinker. He was such an affable fun guy that colleagues did not always appreciate his conceptual mind. He was a model for a lot of us on how to use practice to demonstrate and educate other clinicians.*

Building on early studies of group development that described the beginnings and endings of small groups, Jim and his colleagues analyzed the previously undifferentiated middle phases of group life. Their five-stage developmental model identified predictable patterns in the "closeness" of group members and changes in members' frame of reference over time. During the first stage of pre-affiliation, group members perceive the group from the framework of other experiences in groups or social settings. During the second stage of power and control, and the third stage of intimacy, group members perceive the group from the framework of their families. It is during fourth stage of differentiation that members perceive the group as a unique and distinctive experience, allowing the group to engage in activities with the wider community. The internalized group becomes a frame of reference for future relationships in preparation for the fifth and final stage of separation.

It was Jim's belief that an understanding of group development would help social workers to enhance the social and emotional growth of group members, to appreciate the relationship between the group and its organizational setting, and to evaluate the effectiveness of practice. With the publication of the developmental model, he sought to encourage further research on group development, particularly the applicability of the model to various types of groups and to group work with various populations. To this end, "A Model for Stages of Development in Social Work Groups" (Garland, Jones, & Kolodny, 1965) set a research agenda for Jim Garland's career.

In the course of our oral history interviews, Jim remembered his professional development in stages similar to those in the development of groups. Formative experiences during his youth and early adulthood – experiences that correspond to a pre-affiliative stage – prepared him to enter social work. As he told me (Garland, personal communication, September 15, 1998):

> *I knew what it was like to be a little bit different because I'm half Italian and half WASP. So I had two very different families to associate with and two very different selves. I experienced mixed feelings about class, about being Italian, about being WASP. I was a middle person. I was in the position of being an only child, so I was the mediator between my mother and father. . . You put that all together and that mediating role, and boy, I really landed in the right profession!*
>
> *I was born in 1929, one of the Depression babies. I was always influenced by my parents, and as far back as I can remember, I remember them as having sympathy for the underdog. I'm a working class guy. I live in the town I was born in, Mansfield, Massachusetts. My grandfather was the foreman on the crew that built the sidewalk in front of my house and the fancy stonework on our memorial park. Vincenzo Gaglione was his name, and he changed it, because he was the first Italian in town way back around the turn of the century. He was Vincenzo Gaglione from Naples and he became James Garland.*

When Jim entered Brown University in 1947, he was the first person in his family to go to college. Jim was stunned by the significance of social class at Brown, and he became increasingly aware of the meaning of race and ethnicity in college life. In Jim's words (Garland, personal communication, August 18, 1998):

> *When I started at Brown, the minority group in the academic setting was Jews. I developed a very strong identification with them. It was from Jewish guys that I found a sense of warmth and humor, intelligence, and ability to understand the social and political world. Of course, being a social worker now for forty years, you become at least one-third Jewish, just by being in the profession! But my friendship with Jews fired me up around the question of stereotypes. There were quotas about letting Jews into the Ivy League colleges and there were fraternities that admitted nobody but white Christians. Those were formative experiences, both in terms of my values and in terms of some of the things that I studied, like sociology and psychology.*

Jim's role as a "middle person" and cultural mediator was honed in the Army, as he recalled (Garland, personal communication, August 18, 1998):

When I graduated in 1951, I was drafted. I signed up for three years as an enlisted guy so that I could go to Army Language School. The guy who did the assignments said, "What language would you like?" I said, "French!" – I saw myself going to Paris. He said, "No openings, it's Korean!"

So I studied Korean language and culture for a year at the Army Language School in Monterey, California. It took them long enough to train me that by the time I sailed to the Far East, the war had ended and the Armistice talks were going on. Speaking literate Korean and understanding and respecting Korean culture and customs, I was treated like a king! But I saw the racism of the American soldiers toward Koreans and to a large extent, the racism of Koreans toward Blacks. I felt that I had to do something about that. I wanted to create understanding among people, and I found myself often being a mediator in barracks arguments, occasionally coming to the defense of the Koreans who worked on our post.

I thought about maybe becoming an international diplomat, working in the Foreign Service. But because of my working class background, I didn't see myself being able to succeed at that. I figured I could never get into the Fletcher School of Law and Diplomacy at Tufts. I figured that the next best thing, although I knew very little about either one of them, was to go into social work.

Power and Control Stage: "The Relationship between Social Group Work and Group Therapy: Can a Group Therapist Be a Group Worker, Too?"

On the day of his return from Korea, Jim had his interview at Boston University School of Social Work. Based on Jim's college experiences in athletics and in the arts, the BU faculty steered Jim into the field of group work. As Jim recalled (Garland, personal communication, September 15, 1998):

There's been that balance with me of the dramatic expressive as compared to the traditional male activity. Both of those sides would benefit me when I worked with kids. I understood the use of sports and how to modify them so that they could help regular kids not to feel that they had to become big pros. And I understood that sports could help very shy and timid kids to use assertive motion to have a good time and not to kill somebody. I could do art; I was interested in cooking, which I still am today, and dramatics and outdoor activities and singing. That was what the core of group work was in schools of social work in those days.

At Boston University School of Social Work, Jim began to form his professional identity as a social worker and to transition from the pre-affiliation stage to the "power and control" and intimacy stages of his career. Jim's social work education included group work field placements in settlement house settings, where he led long-term neighborhood groups for socially isolated children and adolescents. In Jim's words (Garland, personal communication, August 18, 1998):

The idea of using activities in the natural place where people lived influenced me very strongly. . . . Group workers used natural surroundings and social activity for growth, for treatment, for support, and for empowerment. The therapeutic approach synthesized psychoanalytic theories and knowledge about psychopathology with sociological ideas about citizenship, normal growth, and the use of social activity.

In addition to his required group work field placements, Jim used his GI benefits to enroll in a summer casework placement at the state psychiatric hospital, which at the time housed 3,500 patients. Upon his graduation from BU School of Social Work in 1956, Jim was hired by Boston Children's Service Association, where he served as a group worker, summer camp director, and director of research. It was here that he collaborated with Hubie Jones, Ralph Kolodny and other colleagues on studying the development of groups. Jim made a radical career change in 1964, when he accepted a position as director of activity therapy at McLean Hospital, the prestigious Harvard-affiliated psychiatric hospital that was "highly psychoanalytic" at the time. As he recalled (Garland, personal communication, August 18, 1998):

My goal was not only to dignify and professionalize the use of activities, but also to put them to service to create a therapeutic milieu in the wards. The other 23 hours outside the psychoanalytic hour would be spent in helping patients to recover from their illness, to take control of their lives, to work on their psychological and interpersonal issues.

Jim became a consultant on ward life, and he integrated psychosocial and systems perspectives with the psychoanalytical framework of the medical staff. After seven years, he felt that he had accomplished his goals at McLean, and in 1971, Jim accepted a faculty position at Boston University School of Social Work. As chair of the Human Behavior sequence, he was charged with integrating sociological and political content into a curriculum that was based on psychoanalytical thought. As he explained (Garland, personal communication, August 18, 1998):

> *At the time, social work students studied human development as interpreted by psychoanalysts, and psychiatrists were our instructors . . . . Little by little I moved aside the psychoanalysts as the major teachers and had social workers teach the courses. We never threw out the analytic material. It became more like ego psychology over the years. But we brought in material on group life in addition to individual life. We brought in material on social role, social class. To me, it was a lesson in how group work can get into the politics of education and help.*

Jim collaborated with students and colleagues in introducing content on human diversity into the human behavior curriculum, including material on race, ethnicity, gender, and sexual orientation. During nearly 30 years at Boston University School of Social Work, he chaired sequences in both Human Behavior and Group Work, served as Acting Dean, and held leadership positions in the university chapter of the American Association of University Professors (AAUP). He also maintained a private group work practice, and assumed state and national leadership roles in the National Association of Social Workers (NASW) and in what was then the Association for the Advancement of Social Work with Groups (AASWG).

Throughout it all, Jim continued to play a mediating role. In his 1986 paper, "The Relationship between Social Group Work and Group Therapy," Jim explored his position as "a man in the middle" as well as the position of group work within the social work profession (Garland, 1986, p. 24):

> *We [social group workers] are truly in the middle position, a mesosystem method in a middle range profession . . . We must play the balance between individual interest and social responsibility. We are still in that place between social education, recreation, and group therapy . . . We are forever in an in-between position searching for our own identity. We are*

the sociologically marginal woman and man boarding in many houses and owning none. In the sometimes unsettling hybrid world of social group work, we can find a dynamic tension, a wellspring of creativity and a strategic position which is often vulnerable to theoretical and political conflicts, but is also in a unique position to promote many kinds of individual and collective change.

Differentiation and Separation Stages: "Loneliness in the Group: An Element of Treatment"

By the mid-1990s, Jim was in demand throughout the Boston area as a consultant to health and human services agencies. Having reached the differentiation stage of his career, he applied the knowledge, values, and skills of social work with groups beyond social work organizations to the greater Boston community. As he remembered (Garland, personal communication, September 15, 1998):

Group work has a real role in organizational consulting, in using group knowledge to understand agency change. As agencies began to grow in size and destabilize because of their growth, or as they were cut back, I began to get more and more requests for consultation that had to do with organizational stress. I came in under situations where there was great personal unhappiness. Sometimes people were being fired and there was a sense of alienation. I could move in where the staff were and deal with them as a group.

In his later career, Jim preferred the intimacy of teaching and consulting to the formality of academic writing, and he left his insights on group work with organizations – such as his distinctions between clinical supervision, clinical consultation, and organizational consultation – to the memories of his colleagues, students, and clients. Although he drew from his understanding of groups to mediate conflicts that arose in his own organizations, such as Boston University School of Social Work, NASW, and AASWG, he never wrote about his use of group work in professional leadership roles.

During our two days together, I felt embraced by Jim's large, gregarious personality, his exuberance, and his appreciation for others. It was easy to imagine how, in times of group stress or conflict, his sense of humor would carry everyone in its tide. A steadfast believer in the place of activities in group work, he brought his ukulele to board meetings. As he said, "I could be direct with people, because they liked me. I played my ukulele all the time." Yet in Jim's view, it was not his outgoing personality that gave him an aptitude for group work, but his ability to be alone. As he told me (Garland, September 18, 1998):

> *I never felt that I completely belonged anywhere. There is something lonely about that, but I could stand being alone; I could stand solitude. And that enhanced my ability to work with groups and to be a consultant, too.*

Of all his publications, Jim considered his 1981 paper, "Loneliness in the Group: An Element in Treatment," to be "the best thing I've written," and a companion to his earlier studies of group development. When Jim and his colleagues had written "A Model for Stages of Development in Social Work Groups" (Garland, Jones, & Kolodny, 1965), they had focused on "closeness" as the central developmental theme. In his later career, after he had survived "the health scares" of prostate cancer and a life-threatening stroke, Jim appreciated loneliness as the other side of closeness and a necessary experience for group members during the group's transitions from one developmental stage to the next. To quote "Loneliness in the Group" (1981, p. 76):

> Social group work, despite its long-standing commitment to helping people to build social relationships, has viewed loneliness primarily as something to be cured . . . [In "A Model for Stages of Development in Social Work Groups,"] my colleagues and I emphasized closeness as the driving force and central theme of the evolving group process . . . We did not elaborate on the possibility that other aspects of group development, embodying both symbiotic and individuating symbolism, might provide for the exploration of both distance and closeness, or that out of the anguish of nonfulfillment might come ego-enriching growth.

Loneliness, Jim believed, is a universal aspect of life and of groups, a resource for creativity, and an experience that group workers may try to avoid. To further quote "Loneliness in the Group" (1981, p. 88):

> It is likely that the popularity of co-leadership in group work . . . is in part

occasioned by anxiety over being different and alone in a crowd . . . The worker should be aware that the lonely stance in the group has potential for increased sensitivity to group and to self and for sharpening the awareness and the understanding of one's professional brokering role.

As he approached retirement, Jim was keenly aware of the process of separation from Boston University, but he felt comforted by the long-term presence of the institutions that he had served and would continue to serve in voluntary or advisory roles. If separating group members look to the social work agency as what Jim called a "forever-transitional object," so Jim remembered the profession of social work with groups. As he wrote in "Loneliness in the Group" (1981, p. 89):

> As the session ends, the worker is left alone to experience loneliness, left by the absence of the group. He or she might entertain two fantasies as one way to evoke a test of how well separation was handled and how well he or she was prepared to help the members use the ending in the service of growth. The first scene is of the group members stopping as they prepare to leave the group room and saying in unison, "We'll never see you again and you didn't do well enough." The second and final scene is of yourself sitting alone in the room for a long time after everyone has left.

The Historical Record

Jim Garland was eager to reach out nationally and internationally to allied professionals, particularly those that practiced group work by other names. In a guest editorial in the *Child and Youth Care Forum* (1994), he remembered hosting European youth workers who identified as social pedagogues. When the visitors expressed concerns about the quality of social work with youth in the United States, Jim passionately agreed (1994, p. 160):

> But what does it mean? Old age and nostalgia? Facing from our admirable visitors how spotty our performance is? Being aware of the schisms and shortcomings of our child and youth practice? Getting another reminder

of the relative diminution of our preventive and health-promoting efforts? Getting a reminder ... of how well we have succeeded in some aspects of conceptual education yet how impoverished we have become, some magnificent field agency programs notwithstanding? Of how far we have drifted away from intimate acquaintance with the daily life of the child and how to enhance it and, with real authority, to teach others how to do it?

In an era when social work seeks evidence-based practice, we sometimes overlook the historical evidence, the experience of practitioners of the past. It was striking to me how difficult it was to find a copy of Jim's often-cited developmental model, "A Model for Stages in the Development of Social Work Groups," which is printed in *Explorations in Group Work,* an out-of-print book by an out-of-business publisher (Garland, Jones, & Kolodny, 1965). A few copies of the book were available through Amazon.com for $159. Fortunately, I had borrowing privileges from an academic library and was able to request a copy of *Explorations in Group Work* through interlibrary loan. Might it be worthwhile for IASWG to make historically significant primary sources on group work freely accessible to all? Perhaps IASWG could secure rights to publish out-of-print resources on its website or in cooperation with other open-source providers. A more difficult challenge is recovering practice wisdom – such as Jim's insights into group work with organizations – that has never made it into print. Might IASWG expand opportunities for publishing oral histories, memoirs, and other biographical and archival materials of group workers, whether in books, sections of journals, or online?

Social workers questioned the future of group work at the first Symposium on Social Work with Groups in 1979, and we are questioning it still (Abels & Abels, 1979). If we take a developmental perspective – and therefore a historical perspective – on our profession, then we find ourselves in the differential stage of development, a time to reflect on our past as we prepare to translate our knowledge and skills to new environments. This is our opportunity to listen to the voices of our own experience and to remember promising practices in social group work that may apply to the radically different yet familiar contexts of the future.

Jim's Recipe for Marinara Sauce

As a part of his life story, Jim offered the recipe for his "world-famous" marinara sauce:

Large can Progresso or Pastene crushed tomatoes
Lots of basil, chopped
Chopped mint
6 cloves garlic chopped
Small box raisins
½ cup good (extra virgin) olive oil
6 oz. Chianti (vino)
Red crushed pepper to taste
Salt to taste
1 lb. linguine
Optional:
1 cup chopped mushrooms
½ cup chopped green peppers
½ cup fennel seeds

In a large frying pan, saute herbs, garlic, mushrooms, peppers, salt, pepper, olive oil. Don't let garlic get brown. Add Chianti and evaporate alcohol. Add tomatoes and simmer, stirring often. Cook linguini in lots of salted, rapidly boiling water. When pasta is *almost cooked*, drain and add it to the sauce. Finish cooking, tossing constantly, serve. Grated cheese optional.

Acknowledgements

Thanks to Jim Garland's former colleagues Hubie Jones and Julianne Wayne, to IASWG, and to participants in the IASWG session, "Remembering Jim Garland," for their insights and support.

References

Abels, S. L. and Abels, P. (Eds.), (1979). *Proceedings of the 1979 symposium on social work with groups.* Louisville, KY: Committee for the Advancement of Social Work with Groups.

Bartolomeo, F. (2009). Boston model. In Gitterman, A. and Slamon, R. (Eds.). *Encyclopedia of social Work with groups* (pp. 103-105). NY: Routledge.

Garland, J. A. (1992). Developing and sustaining group work services: A systemic and systematic view. *Social Work with Groups, 15*(4), 89-98.

Garland, J. A. (1986). Loneliness in the group: An element of treatment. In Glaser, P. H. and Mayadas, N. S. (Eds.). *Group workers at work:Theory and practice in the 80s* (pp. 75-90). Totowa, NJ: Rowman and Littlefield.

Garland, J. A. (1992). The establishment of individual and collective competency in children's groups as a prelude to entry into intimacy, disclosure and bonding. *International Journal of Group Psychotherapy, 42*(3), 395-405.

Garland, J. A. (1986). The relationship between social group work and group therapy. In Parnes, M. (Ed.). *Innovations in social group work: Feedback from practice to theory* (pp. 17-28). NY: The Haworth Press.

Garland, J. A. (1994, June). Social pedagogy, social group work, and the child and youth care field. *Child and Youth Care Forum, 23*(3), 159-160.

Garland, J. A. and Frey, L. A. (1970). Application of stages of group development to groups in psychiatric settings. In Bernstein, S. (Ed.). *Further explorations in group work* (pp. 1-28). Bloomfield, CT: Practitioners' Press.

Garland, J. A., Jones, H., and Kolodny, R. L. (1965). A model for stages of development in social work groups. In Bernstein, S. (Ed.). *Explorations in group work* (pp. 17-71). Boston: Boston University.

Garland, J. A. and Kolodny, R. (1981). *The treatment of children through social group work: A developmental approach.* Boston: Charles River Books.

Garland, J. A., Kolodny, R., and Waldfogel, S. (1962). Social group work as adjunctive treatment for the emotionally disturbed adolescent. *American Journal of Orthopsychiatry, 32*(4), 691-706.

Garland, J. A. and Wayne, J. (1990). Group work education in the field: The state of the art. *Social Work with Groups, 13*(1), 95-110.

Garland, J. A. and West, J. (1984). Differential assessment and treatment of the school-age child: Three group approaches. *Social work with Groups 7*(4), 57-70.

Kayser, J. A. and Morrissey, C. T. (1998). Historically significant memories in social work: Two perspectives on oral history research and the helping professions. *Reflections, 4,* 61-67.

Martin, R. R. (1995). *Oral history in social work: Research, assessment and intervention.* Thousand Oaks, CA: Sage.

Northern, H. (2004). Contributions of Research to Group Work. In Carson, C. J.; Fritz, A. S.; Lewis, E.; Ramey, J. H.; and Sugiuchi, D.T. (Eds)., *Growth and development through group work,* pp. 23-38. NY: The Haworth Press.

Oral History Association (2018). Principles and best practices for oral history Retrieved from http://www.oralhistory.org/about/principles-and-practices/

Index

www.ingramcontent.com/pod-product-compliance
Lightning Source LLC
Chambersburg PA
CBHW062038270326
41929CB00014B/2474